250

# THE WRITER AND HIS WORLD

## LECTURES AND ESSAYS

# THE WRITER
# AND HIS WORLD

*Lectures and Essays*

*By*
CHARLES MORGAN

LONDON
MACMILLAN & CO LTD
1960

MACMILLAN AND COMPANY LIMITED
*London Bombay Calcutta Madras Melbourne*

THE MACMILLAN COMPANY OF CANADA LIMITED
*Toronto*

ST MARTIN'S PRESS INC
*New York*

PRINTED IN GREAT BRITAIN

# PREFACE

CHARLES MORGAN's Essays, collected under the titles of *Reflections in a Mirror* (First and Second Series) and *Liberties of the Mind*, revealed his searching powers as a critic, his depth of sympathy and understanding for the human predicament, and his wide-ranging knowledge of European literature.

After his death there were found among his papers some Lectures and Essays given on various occasions or published in periodicals, but not (with one exception) hitherto presented in book form. These his Executors and his Publishers have now collected under the title of *The Writer and His World*.

A volume of Charles Morgan's Letters, selected and edited by Eiluned Lewis, is in preparation and will be ready for publication some time in 1961.

# CONTENTS

# THE ARTIST IN THE COMMUNITY *

THIS lectureship exists to commemorate one of the most profound and humane of modern scholars, W. P. Ker. It would be appropriate that the lecturer should carry on Ker's work — that he should at all events move within the territory of his criticism; but to do so would require learning that I do not possess, and it has seemed right to me, in my choice of subject, to attempt no more than to move within the province of his independent and fearless spirit.

I

I propose, therefore, to lay before you what I believe to be the next great problem which modern civilization has to face and solve: the problem of how to preserve liberty of thought from the attack of fanatical dogmatism, of how to strengthen the community of freedom against the authoritarian encroachments which now threaten it: in brief, of how to make sure that we and our children live and think and die as men and women, possessing our own minds and souls, and not as a censored and driven regiment with no virtue but obedience.

Next, I shall ask what place an artist has in a free community: what is his duty towards it and what its duty towards him? I shall suggest that the relationship between the

* The sixth W. P. Ker Memorial Lecture delivered in the University of Glasgow 18 April 1945. This is the original text, which differs slightly from the version afterwards published in *Liberties of the Mind*.

artist and the community is, in one aspect, enduring, in that it arises from the nature of art and the nature of society itself; and, in another aspect, constantly changing, in that it arises from changes in artistic practice and in the forms which society assumes in different epochs.

Finally, regarding this relationship between the artist and the community as, in part, constant, and, in part, variable, I shall inquire what the true relationship is now and is likely to become, and shall submit a concluding proposition: That by preserving this true relationship we may help to safeguard the liberty of thought and the community of freedom itself, for an artist is neither the community's priest nor the community's slave, but a member of it who holds in his especial charge certain qualities essential to its spiritual life. He is, as it were, the breath of the people's imagination without which they perish; and the people must learn, in each new phase of history, how to adjust themselves to art, how to receive it, how to make of it an ally with religion and science in every man's quest of truth; how, in each new climate, to breathe freely and deeply; for, if they do not, the authoritarians will stifle them, and the spirit of man, though it cannot die, be cast down, for long centuries, into obscurity and submission. Mrs. Charles Kingsley, in her Life of her husband, spoke a little strangely, as it may now seem to us, of her husband's 'sympathy with Art, and deeper matters'. We may smile at her phrase but at the same time honour her sense of art's relationship to all that she most valued in life. We, in our turn, are called upon to re-gather our strength from Athens and the Renaissance that, after the terrible retrogression which our lives have witnessed, we may prepare a way for what our children or our grandchildren, if they survive, may dare to call the Re-enlightenment.

2

I will, then, attempt, first of all, to state the problem as I
see it. When, in the distant future, historians sit down to
write, what title will they give to the chapter which describes
the second half of the twentieth century? What is life going
to be about?

There are many who say that what lies before us is predominantly an economic struggle, and a few others — too
few, perhaps, for this is a subject which British public
opinion too easily neglects — that our central problem will
be of foreign policy. Both views are reasonable, but they are
evidently interdependent, and there is danger in insisting on
either of them to the exclusion of the other. What is possible
economically depends not upon abstract theory, Marxian or
other, but upon what our international relationships make
possible; and we forget at our peril that foreign policy is the
condition and sanction of home policy, and that security
against foreign enemies is a first charge on social security and
economic advance.

Among the principal subjects with which any historian of
our times will have to deal is our attempt to relate foreign
policy to economic policy and our ability to persuade ourselves, and to persuade others, to accept, for the sake of
gradually establishing an international law, certain limitations upon national sovereignty. That this is the direction
in which peace-loving and unfanatical men will try to move
the world is scarcely open to doubt. But will they be prevented by impatient and bloody extremists? This, I believe,
is the question underlying all the questions of our time. Our
differences of economic theory and foreign policy cannot be
resolved, can scarcely be profitably discussed, until we have

answered within us the personal question: Do I speak and think as a free man or as an authoritarian? Do I wish to live in a free community with men who differ from me in theory and faith, seeking with them — and with other nations — a reconciliation of practice, or am I determined to extirpate, in pursuit of what I believe to be right, whatever faith and theory differs from my own?

Some may feel that this presentation of the alternative is too abrupt. British men and women of my own generation and of a generation older than mine may think so, for we were brought up in an atmosphere and habit of liberty, but the alternative, I am sure, will not be considered too abrupt in France, where the tyrannies and ideologies have stalked into men's homes, or in Poland where — to our own humiliation — the glory of a great nation has been crushed between them, or in Italy where the labour of Garibaldi has been undone, or in Spain where hatred is a poison of the heart; nor, I believe, does the alternative, bitter though it is, seem unreal to Scotsmen and Englishmen of a generation younger than my own. It is to the young I dare to speak, for it is their life, not mine, that will carry the remaining burden of this century, and the Re-enlightenment, if it comes, will be their children's, and perhaps their own, reward.

It was a very young man who first confronted me with this alternative. He was a fighter-pilot, shot down and terribly burned in the Battle of Britain. When he had recovered from his wounds, and the plastic surgeons had rebuilt his face, and he was struggling for that permission to fly again which, being granted, led to his death, he came to dine at my house in London. Through all the bombardments, I had tried to preserve one amenity there: we dined by candlelight and an open fire; and I remember that, after dinner, we went upstairs, I with the decanter and he with the candelabra. I remember it because it was in the upstairs room, just after we had entered it, that he, standing in mid-floor with a candelabrum in each hand, said: 'Nowadays, wherever I go, I ask myself that question about every-body. At dinner, I was asking it about you.' For the moment I had lost his drift. He was carrying on our dinner-table conversation, and I meanwhile had been thinking of other things. 'What question?' I asked. He put down the candelabra and told me, and we talked of it half the night.

His point was this. He felt that everyone in the modern world — everyone, soldier, priest, scholar, tradesman or housemaid — was potentially, whether he knew it or not, either a Communist or a Nazi. 'Potentially,' he insisted. 'As yet, I'm neither myself. But I know which way I'd go if I had to choose. And that's the question I ask myself about other people: which way would they go if they had to choose? Which way *will* they go *when* they have to choose? Which side are they on?'

I said: 'Are they necessarily on either side?'

He answered: 'Yes, I think they are, inside themselves. I think they must be. The world being what it is, a man can't remain an indifferentist.'

That was the word I challenged. It seemed to me false to suggest that the whole area of opinion lying between the two opposing totalitarian polities was indifferent, neutral, colour-less, waiting only to drift helplessly into one or other of the warring armies.

He said: 'That at any rate is the impression that both sides try to give. To a great extent they are succeeding. They are planting the idea that not to be in one camp or the other is a form of uncourageous compromise, and that the whole idea of freedom as a positive force is dead.'

This was the discussion that held us into the night. He assumed that the battle to destroy the community of freedom was over or almost over, and that soon there would be no choice open except between one form of authoritarianism and another. Many in Europe feel as he did. The choice has been thrust upon them. I still believe that, in the long view of history, he and they will be seen to have been wrong. I think that it is in the destiny of the English-speaking peoples and, ultimately, after many vicissitudes, of a recovered France, to prove them wrong. But the other alternative remains. The question may not yet be: 'To which Authoritarianism shall we submit?' Not yet: 'To which slave-master shall we surrender ourselves?' But already and urgently the question is: 'Shall we be bond or free?'

What the fighter-pilot said that night was a young man's evidence that the pressure of authoritarianism was heavy upon him. It is to be felt everywhere in the modern world, in the way in which religion is discussed, in the criticism of art on a basis of politics, in the penetration of common speech by ideological jargon, in the reluctance of so many men and women to defend their own opinion against the attack of extremists. It is to be felt, too, in the tendency, from which few of us are exempt, to be swayed by passing enthusiasms and passing indignations, to reverse our judgement of great issues and even of great nations in accordance with the swaying fortunes of a battle or the flow of some popular emotion, to be carried forward by slogans and headlines rather than by the reasoned development and application of principle. There was alarming evidence of this tendency in our attitude towards the confusion which arose in Athens when the

Germans had gone out. I happen to believe that our Government was right to intervene, but I will not now discuss the merits of that dispute. What was remarkable about it, and relevant to our present subject, was that, when the trouble began, a great part of British opinion, instead of suspending judgement and waiting to ascertain the facts, instead of trying to discover patiently where the true interest of freedom lay, aligned itself hastily on the Left or on the Right, and began to think and talk and write for or against one or other of the authoritarian ideologies. It was as if the minds of the British people had already begun to stiffen, to congeal into two clots of opinion, as if we had begun to lose our independence of judgement, our resilience of imagination, our power to refer each new problem, not to some rigid rule, but to our own consciences, our own sense of compassionate justice. It is the radical principle and the invariable practice of all authoritarian systems to freeze imagination, to prevent men and women from thinking for themselves. It is the radical principle of art to unfreeze the imagination and to enable men and women to think for themselves.

The problem of the future, as I understand it, now lies before you. Let us next consider what part an artist may play, and what part the community may enable him to play, in the solution of it.

### 3

What I am now seeking to discover is whether there are any elements in the nature of art and in the nature of society which may be said to establish an enduring undercurrent of relationship between them. If these elements exist, if they are enduring like the tides, they will be a condition of the relationship between art and society in a particular epoch.

Now if anything in the doubtful history of our race is certain it is that before society existed there were men, and that before schools or coteries or classifications existed there was art. Indeed the first artist was presumably subjective. He made his work of art, his song or the picture he drew on the wall of his cave, in order to express his sense of happiness or fear, or *his* sense of the form of the natural object he depicted. In other words, his art sprang from within him; it was not at first designed to produce an effect upon others; but one day, as he was drawing on the wall to please no one but himself, his wife said: 'My dear, that is not at all my idea of a mammoth. A mammoth, surely, has a longer tail', and so the relationship of art to society was begun. All our aesthetic troubles, and perhaps all our matrimonial troubles, began in that moment, for the first artist, we may be sure, was both flattered and annoyed — flattered because he really had been drawing a mammoth and his wife had recognized it; annoyed because there was, after all, great variety in mammoths and wide scope for the interpretation of them in their relationship to rocks or mountains — it all depended on what *impression* they made upon you — and the first artist thought it unreasonable that his wife should concentrate on the length of the animal's tail. So he said: 'It isn't a mammoth; it's what I feel about a mammoth' — half a lie, half a truth; and she said: 'Well, anyhow, it isn't what I feel about a mammoth. Let us ask Belinda.'

Belinda was their child, and when Belinda saw the picture she thought it was god; she fell down on her face and began to make propitiatory noises; and her father said: 'Well, really, this is too much!' and the man within the artist slapped her soundly. But the artist within the man was flattered, and after a little while he began to say: 'Well, after all, whether I intended it or not, the effect was that I drew Belinda's idea of god. Perhaps that is what art *is*.'

Here, I think, he was right; he had, at any rate, hit upon one aspect of the truth; he had understood the relationship of his art to Belinda. There was, of course, another aspect of the truth, which no doubt troubled him again as soon as he took up another flint and began to scratch on another wall — namely, the relationship of art to himself. Was he trying to reproduce a mammoth or, like Cézanne, to re-present it? Was he giving information about a mammoth, about the length of its tail for example, or was he, in his re-presentation of that debatable animal, giving information about himself? Or was he perhaps not giving information at all? Did he really care what his wife or what Belinda thought? There was a part of him, an extremely important part, that cared nothing for the effect of his drawing upon others or indeed for its likeness to a mammoth or a god; a part of him that was neither zoological nor theological nor social, nor even deliberately self-expressive; a part of him, an impulsive essence, the very seed of art, its innermost mystery, which, without rhyme or reason, said to him: 'Draw!' so that he drew, not for his own sake or for society's sake or for god's sake or even for art's sake, but because something inside him said: 'Draw!'

To this impulse, this absolute of art, many names are given. Some have spoken of it as 'art for art's sake'; some as 'art to the glory of God'; some as a desire for absolute beauty which, to them, is truth and 'a joy for ever'; and in giving to the impulse these names they have unwittingly exposed it to the attack and ridicule of men who neither understand the names nor the thing. Let us beware how we attack or ridicule these names because perhaps to us one or other

B

of them may seem limited or pretentious. Of course they are limited; they are an attempt to express the illimitable. Of course they sound pretentious; they are an attempt to express the inexpressible. Of course foolish cults grow up around them, clinging to the approximate name without having experienced the essential thing. But whatever the name, the impulse of art is holy and absolute as the impulse of love is holy and absolute, not to be traced to its origin, not to be accounted for by its effects, such an inward-feeling and outward-shining glory, such a 'silence within the heart of a cry', as you may see upon the face of Correggio's Io in the moment of her visitation by the god. I wish to establish this ecstatic impulse, neither self-regarding nor world-regarding, as the essence of the artistic act — as it is the essence of the act of love — because, without its saving presence in our minds, we cannot hope to understand rightly the relationship of an artist to the community. A hint of this relationship was given to the first artist when Belinda threw herself upon her face and began to worship not his mammoth but her own god. Towards his wife he had as an artist failed. All she had said was that the animal's tail was too long. Why had he failed? Because in her he had provoked nothing but a slavish desire to have reproduced for her what she had already seen; she wanted repetition and uniformity which, together, are hell, not imagination and variety which are a way to heaven; she was not provoked to a fresh imagining of anything — not even of a mammoth, much less of a god. But with Belinda he had succeeded because by his work of art she had been carried beyond his work of art; it had, so to speak, broken up the coagulation of her mind as a poker thrust into a sleepy fire breaks up the coagulation of the embers; and a flame had jumped out and burned and dazzled her, and the

flame was god. It might not have been god. It might have
been anything — if she had been younger a divine doll, if a
little older an almost divine lover. At all events, it was hers,
not her father's: that is the point. It had grown in her soil,
like a flower from a seed. What her mother had wanted was
what society so often demands of artists — something ready-
made, useful and familiar, something that fulfilled her pre-
conceptions and required of her neither adjustment nor
growth nor imaginative effort of any kind, a clearly recog-
nizable mammoth down to the last inch of its tail. But that
was because the mind of Belinda's mother had become fixed,
frozen, authoritarian, and the art of Belinda's father had
failed to break it up. But with Belinda herself he had succeeded, and, when he had recovered from the shock of having his mammoth taken for a god, he said to himself: 'I
made the girl imagine for herself.' And then he added: 'That
is what art is for. What art *is* is a different matter. I know and
feel that inside myself, and Correggio will know and feel it
when the time comes for him to paint Io in the moment of
her visitation by the god. Meanwhile I know what art is for.
It is to enable men to imagine for themselves.' And he
thought, in saying this, that he had solved the problem of the
relationship of the artist to society, and I think he had taken
a necessary step towards the solution of it; but he had not
solved it, because two vital questions remained unanswered
and the answers to these differ, or appear to differ, from age
to age.

4

These questions are: 'By what means shall an artist
enable men to imagine for themselves?' and, secondly:
'What shall he enable them to imagine?' To the second

question the authoritarian answer is simple: 'The people shall not be enabled to imagine freely. They shall be compelled or persuaded or tempted to imagine what is good for them, and what is good for all is good for one and what is good for one is good for all.' Sometimes the authoritarians dress up this answer in a more dignified and ancient dress, and say: 'The people shall be made to imagine the Truth,' and, when authority says that, we are on the way to the fire and the torture-chamber, to the death of Socrates, to the scourge and the crown of thorns. Why will men torment one another for the kingdom of this world, which is worthless when they have attained it? Why will they torment one another for the kingdom of God, which is within them? If art has anything to teach it is that these torments are vain, and that to mistake one supposed aspect of truth for Truth itself and so to imprison men's curiosity and aspiration in the dungeon of an ideology, is the unforgivable sin against the spirit of man.

An artist is bound by his vocation to recognize as sin the authoritarian's claim to be a monopolist of truth. For that very reason the word truth cannot be excluded from his answers to the two vital questions. When he is asked what he will enable men to imagine, he will answer, in summary: 'Aspects of Truth.' When he is asked by what means he will do this, he will answer, again in summary: 'By communicating my own visions of Truth.' You will observe that the word 'visions' is in the plural: 'visions', not 'vision'; you will remember that Thomas Hardy called a volume of his poems *Moments of Vision* and that he was careful to renounce all claim to a monopoly of truth. 'I have no philosophy,' he wrote, 'merely what I have often explained to be a confused heap of impressions, like those of a bewildered child at a conjuring show.' And you will not have failed to notice that when that giant among artists, Tolstoy, reached that stage of his life which is called his 'conversion'; when, that is to say, he exchanged his many visions of truth for one vision of it and established an ethical system; he became so much the less a practising artist and indeed repudiated art altogether as he had formerly understood it. But Hardy's saying that he had no philosophy is not to be understood to mean that he had no point of view. He stood on a hill-top and from it surveyed experience, and it was his own hill-top; he was not inconsistent in the sense of being without distinct individuality; he was not for ever blown hither and thither by the opinions of others, joining leagues and clubs and fashionable groups and peering out at life through their blinkers. He preserved his integrity, guarded his individua-lity, looked out from his own hill-top. But he did not look only north, or only south, or only east or west. He did not fix upon a favourite view and say: 'This is Truth. There is no other.' He surveyed the whole landscape of experience with what eyes he had, and said to us: 'Look: what do you see with your different eyes?' And we looked, and, though we did not see what he had seen, we saw what we had not seen before and might never have seen but for his visionary flash.

5

What is it then that an artist enables men to see? I think that ideally he enables them, looking out from the point of view of their own individualities, to see their own experience in a light of Truth — in *a* light, not *the* light, for there are many. But the phrase 'in a light of Truth' is a vague one except to the man who uses it. I have used it, and cling to it, because it indicates to me something that is essential to my

idea of the function of art in a community, but I will try to
express in more concrete terms my answer to the question:
'What is it that an artist enables men to imagine?'

An understanding of art's effect upon us, of its real value
to mature men and women, may be reached by trying to
remember what its effect was in childhood. Do you remember, can you still feel, what it was then to fall under the spell
of a book? I remember well how, as I read, a circle seemed
to be woven round me forbidding my thoughts to wander,
so that attention became concentration, and concentration
became at first effortless, then involuntary, then necessitous,
and at last something more — absorption, self-surrender, a
passing into another world. So the spell would fall. But the
world into which I entered was never altogether the author's
world, though I saw it by his light. My own identity was no
more lost than a dreamer's identity is lost during his dream;
but it was, as it were, distilled; what moved in the imagined
world was not I, with the inhibitions of my self-conscious-
ness, but the essence of I, freed from the knowledge that I
was eight years old, or that I had a brother and two sisters,
or that my preparation was not done, or that, if I walked
round the little wood that bordered the tennis-lawn, I should
come to the kitchen-garden: freed, that is to say, from the
relationships of age, of person, of duty, of place, which tied
me in my ordinary life: liberated from my social and tem-
poral bonds, and yet liberated in such a way that I did not
become, in the transition, anti-social, for I was liberated
from my egotistical bonds as well. This was the first part of
the spell — liberation, intensification, purification — a penetration of that film of personality to which name and circumstances are attached — a walking clean through the looking-
glass.

On the other side of the looking-glass was not, as some pretend, an escape from life, but a new impulse and vitality. On this side of the looking-glass we are bound by an unreal sense of order, of partition, of what is congruous and what incongruous; we think of time as if it were a calendar on the wall, each day to be stripped off in turn, the past, the present and the future impenetrable by one another; and this is spiritually untrue; all time is simultaneous; in my end is my beginning. On this side of the looking-glass, we are bound always by a sense that each individuality is locked within itself, so that, even between two people who love each other, though there is communication like the tapping on prison-walls, there is no fusion, and we struggle continually towards this fusion unattainable in this world, giving many names to our struggle; sometimes the name of personal love, sometimes of friendship, sometimes of congregation in the worship of a god, sometimes of society or community. Under the spell of art this separateness may be transcended. On the other side of the looking-glass the prison walls are down. There is inter-penetration of individuality, of time, of place. I well remember that, in childhood, under the spell of a story, I used to feel, without any sense of incongruity, that I myself was present at the Siege of Troy though I remained fully aware that the narrative belonged to the past; on my way home with Odysseus, I found Nausicaa playing ball with her maidens on a stretch of sea-shore where I had bathed yesterday; she had her own face, *and* the face of a beautiful girl whom I knew, *and* a face that was featureless, indescribable, like the face which Michelangelo left unpainted in his unfinished picture, 'The Entombment'; she had many beauties, and, as well, an absolute beauty. And I knew, when I read of the Agony in the Garden, that where Jesus kneeled

to pray was in a corner of the lawn in front of my own house,
just as Giovanni Bellini knew, when he painted the scene,
that Jesus kneeled on a little mound in the midst of an
Italian landscape; and it seemed not unfitting or untrue that,
within two hundred yards of this tennis lawn, was a steep
dell or pit into which Joseph was cast by his brethren; nor
was it unfitting or untrue.

And this breaking down by art of the compartments of
the mind belongs not only to childhood. I first read Keats's
'Eve of St. Agnes' when I was a young naval officer in the
China Seas. My mind accepted the poet's description of his
scene — the ancient castle, the bloodhound at the gate, the
painted glass of the upper room.

> Full on this casement shone the wintry moon
> And threw warm gules on Madeline's fair breast,
> As down she knelt for heaven's grace and boon;
> Rose-bloom fell on her hands, together prest,
> And on her silver cross soft amethyst,
> And on her hair a glory, like a saint:
> She seem'd a splendid angel, newly drest,
> Save wings, for heaven —

For me then, for me now, full on this casement shines the
wintry moon, and yet, at the same time and with an enhance-
ment, not a dissipation, of the illusion, it shines also into a
cabin of H.M.S. *Monmouth* at sea, in which cabin for ever
Madeline sleeps.

That is the spell — not in this room, not in this large
company, but in the cabin of the *Monmouth* at sea, that was
the spell which broke down the divisions of time, place and
circumstance, and set the spirit free to go on its voyages.
The greatest tribute that a writer earns from us is not that
we keep our eyes fast upon his page, forgetting all else; but
that sometimes without knowing that we have ceased to

read, we allow his book to rest, and look out over and beyond it with newly opened eyes, discovering all else. Then lies open to earthbound man the firmament of the spirit; he takes wing and travels in it, liberated from the chains of partial judgement and from the blindness of close appearances. Like a bird released from a cage, he soars, and sees truth in new aspects. And though the spell of art breaks at last and he returns to earth, it is not to the cage of his former prejudice that he returns. The spell of art breaks, the 'Eve of St. Agnes' is ended; the young officer finds himself in the cabin again, feels the throb of engines, listens to the whirr of an electric fan. It is five minutes to eight bells, and he goes on to the bridge to keep his middle-watch. But he has been a liberated spirit, and thereafter, in all life's embittered divisions, in all his faults and follies and self-imprisonments and hardnesses of heart, he never altogether ceases to be aware of the unity of the living with the dead, and in all his temptations to hatred or fear he cannot be without compassion. Art has planted in him a seed from which his own imagination shall spring; has fertilized his earth that of it he may be reborn. An artist does not renew society; he enables men to renew themselves and so, in the long run, the society in which they live.

6

In saying this, in suggesting what an artist may enable men to imagine, I have, perhaps, already implied an answer to the other vital question: how does an artist produce this effect? I shall not here elaborate that answer, for I do not wish to plunge into a discussion of technical processes or into a matching of one school with another. I seek a common factor, and this much, I think, is clear: that if the true effect of art is to enable men to re-value their own experience in terms of the absolute values — that is to say, in terms of Compassion, Beauty and Truth — the artist himself must value life in those terms and must be able to communicate his valuation in a way that is not merely a statement of his opinion or even an account of his vision but is fertilizing.

This view of the function of art receives endorsement as soon as we ask ourselves what the difference is between a good book, important in its own age, and an immortal book which has continuing life in generation after generation. When you and I read the *Decameron* of Boccaccio or the Sonnets of Shakespeare or Emily Brontë's *Wuthering Heights*, our pleasure and excitement are not the same as the pleasure and excitement in which these masterpieces were written. We are different creatures, nurtured in a different age, and what we imagine is not what those dead writers imagined. In brief, their books are alive because their life is renewed in us, because we re-imagine them; and their genius consists in their power to enable us to do so, in their fertilizing power. They are not beautiful flowers pressed in an album; they seed, and, though they die in one generation of men, they bring forth in another. So Keats, who was far removed from Boccaccio and did not see what he saw, was nevertheless inspired by a story of Boccaccio's to write 'Isabella, or The Pot of Basil' and we, reading 'Isabella', though we do not see what Keats saw, are impregnated by his vision to bring forth our own.

Now if we agree that, from the point of view of the community, what is important in an artist is his impregnating-power, and that, from the point of view of an artist, what is important in the community is its power to be impregnated and to re-present his vision in an eternal vitality and fresh-

ness, does it not follow in the first place that the subject of a
work of art, though important, has not, and cannot have, the
primary importance that a part of modern criticism, and
particularly authoritarian criticism, is inclined to attach to it?

The subject of a story or a poem (and I continue to speak
in terms of literature, though the same principle may be
applied to the other arts), the subject of a story or a poem is
evidently important because neither story nor poem can
exist without a subject; but the subject is not the essence or
the immortal, fertilizing quality of the work of art, but a
limitation upon it. No one, unless he is a historian in quest
of material, now reads Dickens because he wrote about
prison-reform or Turgenev because he wrote about liberal-
ism in Russia or Victor Hugo because he attacked Napoleon
the Third; and no one in the future will read Mr. Wells
because he once chose as his subject certain doctrines of the
Fabian Society. Or, rather, people may *read* these authors
because they are interested now or in the future in subjects
related to these subjects, but their own imaginations will not
be fertilized by the subject — for then any pamphlet would
serve as well — but by the excitement with which the
author wrote about the subject. The fertilizing power is not
the subject, but the aesthetic passion which the author pours
into it; and this aesthetic passion is expressed not in subject
alone or in treatment alone but in a harmony between them.
Therefore we are not to say except at the peril of an ultimate
sterility: 'This subject is admissible, that subject is barred',
or: 'This treatment is admirable, that treatment is ruled out',
and this is precisely what the authoritarians of all ages do say.
It is madness and folly for us to cry: 'But we are modern.
Our particular brand of authoritarianism really is right. Our
preference for free verse — or what you will — really is the

last word in prosody. Our particular swerve towards ecclesiasticism or proletarianism or romanticism or realism — or what you will — really is the law and the prophets.' In saying this, we are ourselves committing all the sins which we condemn in others as we read the history of literature. We say of Victorian criticism that it insisted too much on the religious or ethical content of the work it criticized. And so it did. But it knew what it was doing; according to its lights it could sometimes be wonderfully fair, and we find that when Mrs. Humphry Ward published *Robert Elsmere*, a novel which struck to the very heart of Victorian religious controversy, *The Spectator* could say:

> Profoundly as we differ from Mrs. Humphry Ward's criticism of Christianity we recognize in her book one of the most striking pictures of a sincere religious ideal that has ever yet been presented to our generation under the disguise of a modern novel.

How many modern reviews are there which, being wedded to one or other of the authoritarian ideologies or even to one of our slightly less ferocious economic 'isms', would thus praise on its merits the work of a writer from whom they 'profoundly differed'? It is within the recollection of you all how, in the period between this war and the last, a powerful section of criticism looked upon certain subjects and certain treatments with such horror that they were excluded from discussion and from the anthologies. With the exception of one unrepresentative poem about Clouds, Rupert Brooke was completely shut out from Yeats's *Oxford Book of Modern Verse*; his war poems and his love poems were treated as if they were obscene. In the same volume another poet of the same generation, Robert Nichols, is given a place, but his war poems also are unrepresented.

Yeats would not give room to this, which will live when two-thirds of the poems he included are forgotten:

> Was there love once? I have forgotten her.
>   Was there grief once? Grief yet is mine.
> O loved, living, dying, heroic soldier,
>   All, all, my joy, my grief, my love are thine!

And if Yeats, a great poet, compiling not a personal anthology but an Oxford book, could be thus cabined by a partisan distaste for certain subjects and treatments, how much fiercer and narrower was the partisanship of the camp-followers whose very livelihood depended upon their closely following the camp! They took the view that art should, in its subject, reflect what Yeats calls their 'social passion' and what I should call their political fanaticism. They insisted further that certain treatments, certain ways of writing, should be regarded as the brand of Cain. They howled against romanticism as Victorian spinsters howled against sex.

> Great Heaven! When these with clamour shrill
>   Drift out to Lethe's harbour bar
> A verse of Lovelace shall be still
>   As vivid as a pulsing star.

The verse is William Watson's, and Yeats himself quoted it in his preface to the *Oxford Book*. How strange that he should quote it and himself fall into the very error that it condemned!

No: we are not to dictate to an artist either subject or treatment, nor are we to deny to him any subject or any treatment. We are not schoolmistresses. We are not censors. All that matters is that the subject be one that awakes the artist's aesthetic passion, and that the harmony between subject and treatment be such that it casts a spell upon him, enabling him to be visited by his god, and so casts a spell upon us, enabling us to be visited by ours. 'The excellence of every art,' said Keats, 'is — ' What a wonderful beginning of a sentence! If the page of Keats's manuscript had ended there and the next page been lost, the world would have been breathless to know how the sentence continued. 'The excellence of every art,' said Keats, 'is —' and he did not say that it was in its subject or in its treatment, still less that it was in its social passion or its adherence to any ethical system or in its contemporaneousness. 'The excellence of every art,' said Keats, 'is its intensity.' And what did he mean by that? Fortunately he tells us. 'Capable,' he continues, 'of making all disagreeables evaporate from their being in close relationship with Beauty and Truth.' Do not misunderstand him. By 'disagreeables' he does not mean things that are unpleasant to us; he means those things which do not agree together, which clash in our immediate experience, but which harmonize when seen in the aspect of eternity. Keats's 'disagreeables' are what I have called our incongruities, of time, of place, of individuality, of right seemingly opposed to right, of loyalty conflicting with loyalty. It is the function of art by its intensity to penetrate these incongruities, to perceive some aspect of order in the chaos of living, some aspect of beauty in that order, some aspect of truth in that beauty, and so to distil experience that we are made partakers of its essence and are enabled to re-imagine it and to renew ourselves.

7

It would seem then that though, as I suggested at the outset, art continually changes its practice and society its forms so that to us, who float upon the surface of experience, there appears to be a variable relationship between them, and though, in a sense, the relationship *is* variable and we have continually to adjust ourselves to it, the adjustments we make should always be so designed as to preserve the true and essential relationship. This willingness to see the artist as an impregnator of the spirit of man and not as a propagator of his own, or our own, opinions, is of the more importance in a period of swift and radical social change. The tendency of our time is for human thought, alarmed by the rapidity of change, by the seeming dissolution of society into a condition of flux, to congeal into stiff, uniform chunks of fierce and frightened orthodoxy — the orthodoxy which condemned Keats because he did not write like Pope, the orthodoxy which condemned Swinburne because he was unchristian, the orthodoxy which in our own day invented the ignorant word 'escapist' and pretends that social consciousness is the criterion of art. And so we are in danger of demanding, as authoritarians do, that an artist fall in with our platoon, or of insisting that he must be in our sense a good citizen before we will regard him as a good artist. In fact it is probably desirable that an artist should be, as a man, a good citizen; that he should obey the laws and fight his country's enemies and care for the happiness of the people. It is probably desirable that he should do these things because, if he does them, the experience may be valuable to him, and, if he does not, he may fall into opposition to the State and waste his energies either in exile or in struggles important to him as a man but irrelevant to him as an artist. But though good citizenship may be desirable to him, it is evidently not always so; certainly we are not qualified to define good citizenship for him and to reject him, as an artist, because as a man he does not conform to our definition. Do we condemn Thomas Mann because by Nazi standards he has not been a good citizen of his own German State? Do we exclude Shelley because, as a citizen, his behaviour was extremely odd? No: we may enforce our laws upon the man but not our opinions upon the artist. And he, in his turn, must understand that, though he is entitled to express his opinions, he is no more entitled to drill the community than the community is entitled to drill the artist in him. He is entitled to express his opinions if the subject of those opinions is what at the moment stirs his aesthetic passion; in this way, great religious poetry has been produced; but woe to him if his art does not transcend his didacticism and carry him away from it and beyond it! Woe even to Shelley if he had not so often and so gloriously forgotten to be a propagandist! Immortality is not to be voted at a political meeting. Posterity will not stay in any man's school. We are wilful and enchanted children, by the grace of God. Our school-classes and our school-books and our school-rewards and punishments matter very little to us in the end. For an hour or two we may earnestly concern ourselves with them, and turn our solemn, communal eyes on the teacher who presides over these things; but what in our heart of hearts we want to know about is the world beyond this class-room of his. He whom we love and remember is not he who thrusts upon us his own dusty chart of the Supreme Reality, scored over with his arguments, prejudices and opinions; nor he who will draw a map of heaven on the blackboard and chastise us with scorpions if we will not fall down and worship it; but he who will pull the curtain away from the class-room window and let us see our own heaven with our own eyes. And this enablement of mankind I take to be the function of true education, for the very word means a leading-out, and to lead out the spirit of man, through the wise, liberating self-discipline of learning and wonder, has been the glory of great teachers and of great Universities since civilization began to flower.

We are citizens, but we are men and women; we are men and women, but we are spirits. We live in the spirit, though we are instructed in the mind —

> The mind, that ocean where each kind
> Does straight its own resemblance find;
> Yet it creates, transcending these,
> Far other worlds and other seas.

And to these, and to the truth that dwells in them, we come not by instruction but by vision, the vision that penetrates to the spirit through the senses. Shelley knew; he stopped preaching and drew attention to something that was not a bird and far transcended the skylark. Keats knew: he did not preach at all, and in his vision forgot even the nightingale. And Hardy knew:

> Love is, yea, a great thing,
>     A great thing to me,
> When, having drawn across the lawn
>     In darkness silently,
> A figure flits like one a-wing
>     Out from the nearest tree:
> O love is, yes, a great thing,
>     A great thing to me!
>
> Will these be always great things,
>     Great things to me? . . .
> Let it befall that One will call,
>     'Soul I have need of thee':
> What then? Joy-jaunts, impassioned flings,
>     Love, and its ecstasy,
> Will always have been great things,
>     Great things to me!

So let us not, ladies and gentlemen, think too communally on the relationship of the artist and the community, for along

c

that path of thought lie the gauleiters on the one hand and
the commissars on the other. What then? As you like it or
what you will.

> ... Joy-jaunts, impassioned flings,
> Love, and its ecstasy ...

skylarks, nightingales! Take them, but take them into yourselves. Give the artist freedom that he may discover; preserve yourselves in freedom that you may receive and re-
create. Go out and find him. You will recognize a true artist
easily enough nowadays, for he will not be wearing a party-
badge:

> 'Tis the man who with a bird,
> Wren, or Eagle, finds his way to
> All its instincts; he hath heard
> The Lion's roaring, and can tell
> What his horny throat expresseth
> And to him the Tiger's yell
> Comes articulate and presseth
> On his ear like mother-tongue.

That is the artist. You are the community. Lions and
skylarks, tigers and nightingales, eagles and wrens, love and
its ecstasy — all are subjects of art and all are at your dis-
posal. But do not conscribe them. Do not bring them into
the classroom and stuff them and stick labels on them — for,
to do that, you must kill them first. Go out and find them.

The lecture, thank heaven, is over. The specimens are all
packed away in their boxes. Shall we go out into Vanity Fair,
and tell stories, or live them? The classroom door is open, as
in a free University the classroom door always is, but let us
beware of the fierce, solemn little men who say that they
have been given the keys.

# THE INDEPENDENCE OF WRITERS *

Is it not a strange world, this world in which it has become necessary for an Englishman to travel to Europe in order to defend the independence of writers? Sometimes it seems to me that we have entered into a period of pure fantasy. Everything is topsy-turvy. *Tout est sens dessus-dessous.* The most extreme dictatorships speak of themselves as democracies. The most eager revolutionaries advocate a system so rigid and regimented that by comparison with it the system of Metternich was a field of wild flowers. Thus far has liberty travelled since 1848.

In the past, the apostles of freedom, Byron and Shelley, came to Geneva in order to escape the tyranny of the Right. Today I come to Geneva in order to defend liberty against the attacks of the Left.

It is tragic fantasy because those who attack liberty today are often those very intellectuals who were formerly eager in its defence. They are overwhelmed by a passion for uniformity, and are unfortunately followed by many innocent dupes. There are many in the world who do not in the least understand what has happened. There are many with generous, progressive and liberal minds who have a fixed idea, inherited from the past, that the men of the Extreme Left are still on the side of progress and generosity. It is no

* A lecture delivered at *Rencontres internationales de Genève*, September 1948.

27

longer true. From what quarter does the attack upon liberty come? The answer is that I, who am neither a Communist nor a Socialist, nor a politician at all, am here to defend liberty. I was a naval officer, I am a story-teller. Politics is not in my blood.

First of all, we must consider the meaning of the word *s'engager*. Does it mean to be devoted, to be dedicated? If that is its meaning; if it means that art is dedicated, as all spiritual acts are dedicated, to the service of powers greater than the powers of this world; if, in brief, an artist *qui s'engage* is one who submits himself to his inspiration, then I have no quarrel with the word. But that is not the sense in which it is commonly used today. If *s'engager* means to enlist in a regiment; if the suggestion is that an artist should submit his inspiration to any earthly power or interest, then it is an enemy word. An artist has no masters except God and Nature. Under them, he is free.

And yet everywhere today the attack upon his freedom is persistent. Sometimes it is ferocious and is supported by all the machinery of a police-state; sometimes, in countries which still enjoy a measure of political freedom, it is discreet and insinuating; always and everywhere it is persistent and plausible. Why is this? Why do so many people throughout the world wish to destroy a writer's independence? It is necessary that we should do our utmost to understand, and to represent justly, opinions which differ from our own.

Those who wish to destroy the independence of writers appear to be of two kinds. Some are, consciously and deliberately, men of violence, men of blood; they are the gangsters of the modern world. They desire disorder that, out of disorder, their tyranny may emerge. They are opposed to the healing of society, and hate the independence of art because they fear its spiritual and healing power. No one can listen to the slow movement of Mozart's Quintet in G minor or to Chopin's Third Étude, Opus Ten, or look at Giovanni Bellini's 'Agony in the Garden', or read Turgenev's *First Love* without being filled with emotions of gentleness and compassion which, if they prevailed throughout the world, would deprive the men of violence of their opportunity. I shall not pause to discuss the evil by which they are inspired.

But there is a second group who wish to destroy the independence of artists but are nevertheless to be thought of as men of goodwill. Though I differ from them profoundly, it is my duty to see the problem with their eyes.

Their argument is this. Artistic independence has produced great works in the past of which they admit the value. They admit also that the critical power of the pen, exercised in opposition to received opinion, has led to desirable changes in human thought. But, they say, the time for that is over. Artistic independence is individualism in its most intense form, and individualism in any form is opposed to the general movement of the world. There is no longer any need of it. Mankind is moving towards collectivism. It is driven in that direction by economic necessity, and it seems to them that an artist who refuses to enlist his art in the service of the collective State is guilty of two errors: first, he is opposing himself to the Zeitgeist; secondly, he is a traitor or 'escapist', as a soldier is who deserts from the army.

Then there are other men of goodwill, who, though they do not endorse the extreme coercive attitude which I have just described, nevertheless take a utilitarian view of art. They ask what *good* it does to the majority of men. Evidently it does not provide them with food or drink or clothing. Of what use is it, then, if it does not instruct them? And if an artist's duty is to instruct men for their own good, does it not follow, they ask, that he must throw in his lot with one or other of the political parties which, each in accordance with its own lights, are trying to improve society? The utilitarians and the extreme collectivists differ from one another in an important respect: the extremists say that art must be the servant of one party, which alone is guardian of the truth; the utilitarians say, a little more generously, that art may choose its party; but they unite in believing that, in the modern world, an independent artist is an anachronism.

I have tried to state the argument of my opponents as fairly as I can. I shall now proceed first of all to examine it; then, turning aside from defence, to carry the attack into the enemy's camp.

2

Those who believe that it is a writer's duty to enlist his pen in the service of the State rest their case upon two ideas which are essentially false. The first of these false ideas is that each man is a consistent unit and exists wholly as a citizen. The second is that the State is a mystical source of life to which men owe a natural and all-inclusive allegiance. None of this is true.

A man is not a consistent unit. He has many aspects. In each aspect he has differing duties, and it is the charm, the peril and the glory of our life that these duties conflict continually, but may be harmonized. For example: one man may be the father of a family and have a duty to his wife and children; he may be an Englishman and have a duty to his King; he may be a Christian and have a religious duty; he may be a man of science and have a duty to seek knowledge for its own sake. Suppose, for a moment, that he is a physicist engaged in atomic research. Is it not clear that his duties may conflict? Is anyone prepared to say that his whole duty is that of a citizen and that he is morally bound to pour his whole energy into the making of atomic bombs in order to increase the power of the State? If he is not bound to do this, then neither is a writer bound to enlist his pen in the service of the State. The scientist must, as a citizen, perform the duties common to all citizens; he must pay his taxes and obey the law; but nothing requires him, as a man of science, to direct his search for pure knowledge into channels convenient to the State. As a citizen, but only as a citizen, his duty is to the State. As a man of science, his duty is to pure knowledge. A writer is no more bound to write propaganda, even in time of war, than a scientist is bound to make atomic bombs. Each has his duty to the State; each has a separate duty to his art or his science.

The unitary idea of man which I am now attacking might also be called the totalitarian idea of man. It is the idea that each one of us is a total unit. It is opposed to all the teachings of psychology and of religion. Is it not opposed also to the experience of each one of us? 'One man in his time plays many parts,' said Shakespeare, and we know by our own experience that we play many parts *at the same time*. Is there anyone in this room who feels that he or she is *wholly* a citizen? Are you not a man? Are you not a woman? Are you not a scientist, a writer, a painter, a teacher? Are you not a lover? Are you not a Catholic or a Protestant? Are you not aware of distinct capacities, distinct loyalties, and so of distinct duties within yourselves?

The totalitarians reply that this constitutes an intolerable division of the human personality. They say that, whether we are artists or scientists, Catholics or Protestants, we are, above all, citizens and must surrender all our capacities to the State. This is utterly false. It is upon the idea of distinct capacities within ourselves that the integrity of the human personality rests. They who say otherwise are like those Pharisees who came to Jesus wishing to entangle him and said: "'Is it lawful to give tribute unto Caesar or not?" But Jesus perceived their wickedness and said, "Why tempt ye me, ye hypocrites? Shew me the tribute money." And they brought unto him a penny. And he saith unto them, "Whose is this image and superscription?" They say unto him, "Caesar's." Then saith he unto them, "Render therefore unto Caesar the things which are Caesar's; and unto God the things that are God's."'

This is the ultimate statement of the doctrine of Distinct Capacities. A writer is to render to the State the things which are the State's, that is to say the duties which he has in common with all citizens; but he is to render to his art the things that are his art's.

### 3

I turn now to the second argument — namely that the State is, in the philosophical sense, a reality; and that, in itself, it is entitled to devotion or piety. My answer will be that the State is not a reality but an expedient — a means of living together from which we derive certain advantages and to which we owe certain duties; but these duties, though they may require us to die in war, are not mystical or religious; they do not require us to surrender our souls to the State or to identify ourselves with it.

The quasi-mystical view of the State is of profound interest. Very few philosophers have been altogether free of it. It clearly affected works as widely different as the *Republic* of Plato, the *Contrat Social* of Rousseau and the *Leviathan* of Hobbes. Marx revived it in a new form, substituting the international community of a class for the earlier ideas of the City State or the National State. Since Marx, the idea has found new expression among Nazis and Communists.

The root of the idea is always this: that an association or community of men, in one form or another, constitutes a reality more profound than the reality of an individual man. The question is: Shall we think of ourselves as existing *in* the community? Shall we say: 'I am because the community is'? Or shall we think of the community as existing because we have made it, and say: 'The community *is* because we are'?

In giving our answer we are bound to distinguish as far as we can between the promptings of our reason and of our emotion. We are all inclined by nature not only to rational- ize our emotions, but to emotionalize our reasons. So it happens that the human mind, when it thinks of the com- munity or of any collective group, raises up a symbol to represent that group. Sometimes that symbol is a flag, some- times a party, sometimes a class, sometimes a king. We shall never reach a true judgement in these matters until we re- cognize that our own symbols are highly emotional, and that other men's symbols, which may seem to us ridiculous or wicked, are as valid for them as ours are for us.

I recognize in myself a symbolic loyalty (which is in effect a *mystique*) to my King. I know that, if I had lived in the seventeenth century when there was civil war in Eng- land, I should have fought for the King, and I still regard the killing of King Charles I as murder. What are my reas- ons for this? There are many good reasons: for example, that the killing was illegal or that, in my opinion, monarchy is, in England, the most expedient form of government. These reasons support my royalism, but I fully recognize that they are not the spring of it. It is, at root, emotional. Therefore, I am bound to recognize the emotional loyalties of other men however wrong I may think them.

Nevertheless if I acknowledge, then my opponents must acknowledge in their turn, that there are limits to even symbolic loyalties. There are areas of life which they do not affect. My loyalty to the King affects my action as a citizen; it does not affect my liberty of thought. The King may order me to fight and I shall obey, but he cannot make me believe anything that I do not in myself believe. He may order me to pay a tax and I shall pay it, but he cannot make me think that the tax is just if my reason tells me that it is unjust. If the King were to order me to falsify my art, I would die rather than obey. I do not for a moment acknowledge that I exist in him. I do not identify myself with him. I have an individual existence which is independent of him. So does every man, however great his emotional and symbolic loyalty to a class or to a State, have an individual existence independent of his class and his State. He is not identified with it. Even if we exclude from our consideration *la vie intérieure*; even if we put aside that relationship between man and God to which atheists deny validity; even if we agree to think in terms of the senses only; still there remains what Montesquieu calls *la conduite intérieure*. This is independent of the State, of class, of King, of community. The art of writing, like all art, is an interior process of the mind. It is part of *la conduite intérieure*. Community, class, State and King are external to it. Any claim by the community to absorb it is therefore irrational.

We have then, I think, reached the same conclusion by two converging paths. We have seen that man is a creature of distinct capacities who is called upon to render unto Caesar only those things which are Caesar's; and we have seen also that the State is not a mystical body but a more or less expedient organization. The conclusion is that the State has no moral right to insist that a man identify himself with it or that an artist surrender to it those parts of his life which belong to *la conduite intérieure*.

4

Another question now arises. Is a writer to be free to write whatever he pleases? Is he entitled to say that, because his writing is part of *la conduite intérieure*, the State must not control it in any way? The answer is clearly that a degree of control is necessary. The artistic process is part of *la conduite intérieure*, but publication is a public act, and falls within the area of law. A writer, for example, cannot be allowed, in his writings, to persecute and defame innocent citizens; they must be protected and there must be a law of libel to protect them.

This is a limitation upon the independence of writers which I accept. We may think that, in some countries, for example in England, the law of libel is too strict, and in other countries, for example in the United States, not strict enough, but we are generally agreed that a law of libel is necessary. Are there any other limitations upon the freedom of writers to which we may consent?

I think that, in certain circumstances, there are. For example, in time of war, the State is entitled to prohibit the publication of information valuable to the enemy. Having admitted this, we are not far from admitting that, in periods of emergency, the State is entitled to prohibit writing dangerous to its own security, and such an admission might open the door to gross tyranny. Who is to define the emergency? Who is to say what is 'dangerous'? The answer is practical, not theoretical. In practice, when there is a free and balanced constitution, these questions are reasonably answered, but where there is a totalitarian government or government by a single chamber they are tyrannically answered. A balanced constitution is as necessary to protect the fundamental liberties from the tyranny of the ballot-box as it is to protect them from the tyranny of a despot. The freedom of writing is in constant peril wherever there is not what Montesquieu called *une séparation des pouvoirs*, and a group of tyrants or an unchecked democratic majority is able to suppress opposition. If writing is to be free, it is above all necessary that its freedom should not lie at the mercy of men who temporarily hold the reins of government. *Il faut que, par la disposition des choses, le pouvoir arrête le pouvoir.*

But if we once admit that, in certain circumstances, there may be limits imposed upon the independence of writers, we are called upon to distinguish, if we can, the principles that should guide the State in the exercise of its powers.

There are, I think, three principles of value:

*First*: There should be no restraint of writing on moral or religious grounds, for this is to trespass on *la vie intérieure*.

*Second*: There should be no restraint of writing on the ground that it criticizes the government in power unless it can be shown in a court of law independent of the government that the writing was treasonable or seditious in purpose and in effect.

*Third*: That though a negative restraint upon writing may, in certain emergencies, be justifiable, a positive requirement of writers by the State is always evil.

5

This final principle needs a little elaboration. My whole case rests upon it. Let me restate it. The law may sometimes say to a writer: 'You shall not', but it is never entitled to say: 'You shall'. A positive censorship, a censorship which requires all writers to conform to a prescribed theory, to *s'engager*, is the damnable thing.

It is this positive censorship, this damnable thing, that many of my opponents advocate today — often without knowing it. In avowedly totalitarian countries, it is openly advocated. In Russia men are not only forbidden to write in opposition to the régime; they are required to write prose, poetry and even music in support of it. The same principle of positive censorship was active in Nazi Germany. I well remember that, when I was in Munich in 1934, I asked a high official what was the attitude of the régime towards Goethe and Schiller. I was told that Schiller was approved; on the subject of Goethe the official was painfully and resolutely silent. I asked then what would be the attitude of the régime towards a new work of art, a play or a poem, that was completely unpolitical — to a new love-story, for example, that was as unpolitical as Shakespeare's *Romeo and Juliet*. I was told that it would be frowned upon. I asked: 'Why? Why should it be frowned upon if it did not in any way criticize the régime?' The answer was: 'Because we feel that all artists should actively support the new Germany and that any artist who does not do so is a traitor by avoidance.' That is positive censorship. It is applied today not only by governments in totalitarian countries but by coteries and committees in countries nominally free. The first question they ask of an artist is: what is his *Weltanschauung?*

Now, there are today many men of goodwill, not themselves totalitarians, who advocate this principle. They express it a little differently. They do not say that an artist who writes an unpolitical love-story is 'a traitor by avoidance', but they do say that he is an 'escapist'; they do not say that he must actively support 'the new Germany', but they do say that he must show himself to be actively interested in what interests them — namely what they are pleased to call 'the development of new thought' or 'the progress of social justice' or 'the modern movement of the world-mind'. It does not matter what phrase they choose. Their purpose is always the same: to compel an artist to be a supporter of their particular ideology, and to exile and persecute him if his works of art do not declare him to be an advocate of their *Weltanschauung.*

This positive censorship, this attempt of critics, banded together for that purpose, to compel artists to choose a particular range of subjects and to display a particular attitude of mind towards them, is, in my view, the greatest evil by which the thought of Western Europe is threatened today. I say 'Western Europe' because to the east of the Iron Curtain the cause of freedom is temporarily lost. I say 'temporarily' because, as long as freedom survives in the West, there is always hope that it may be recovered in the East. But it will not be recovered, and will utterly perish throughout the world, unless we recognize that to require an artist to have any particular *Weltanschauung* is an evil to be resisted at all costs.

## 6

Hitherto I have drawn your attention to the arguments of my opponents. I will now make a positive statement of my own faith in this matter.

First, all subjects are permissible in art. An artist is entitled, he is indeed bound, to choose a subject which deeply moves him. If that subject is political, I would not deny it to him; nor must he deny unpolitical subjects to me. If what interests and moves him is some aspect of 'modernism', by all means let him write of it; if what interests and moves me is the enduring tragi-comedy of human nature rather than a specifically modern aspect of it, let me write of it. The true basis of criticism is never Subject. Nor is the true basis of criticism Style. The true basis of criticism is the harmony of Style with Subject, of Form with Vision.

Vision is the key-word. It is often said by honest men, who know no better, that they cannot understand how any modern artist can fail to be interested primarily in politics or, at any rate, in sociology. This, they say, is a political and sociological age, and there must be something wrong with an artist whose natural choice of subject is not political and sociological. They feel that such an artist is too aloof, that he is not making the contribution which he ought to make to the service of mankind.

The answer is that they are confusing art with journalism. They are confusing vision with persuasion. It may or may not be desirable to persuade men to take certain actions or to think certain thoughts or to hold certain opinions. Whether or not this is desirable, it is not an artist's business.

I believe that an artist's duty is first of all to understand that the Kingdom of *his* god is within him. He is to become more and more intensely aware of this; he is to learn himself, to cultivate his interior vision, and strive continually to distinguish, in himself, his *Being* from the appearances of his life.

Next, he observes the world. He observes its confusions and its strange tranquillities, its doom of suffering and its desperate beauty. He becomes aware of its mystery, namely this: that, though men exist in communities, they live, each one, alone. On this earth each man wears the armour of his separate identity. Never, while he lives, can he take it off. His contact with other men is a contact of armour against armour. There is, on the level of appearance, no naked communication between man and man.

An artist perceives that it is the function of his art to penetrate the armour of appearances and by its vision to enable vision in others. That is his supreme service to men. Not to persuade or compel or instruct them. Not to tell them what their vision shall be. But by his vision, by his power to penetrate the appearances of things, to demonstrate to men that there is such a thing as vision; that there is, within appearances, a truth to be sought for; that within the stiff, hard armour which divides man from man there is a naked communication of which human love is the symbol; that within the discords of this life there is an interior harmony of which we become aware when, observing Nature and knowing her ferocity, we are overwhelmed by the innocence of a flower or the stillness of a mountain. The duty of an artist is not to impose his vision upon men but to open their eyes; not to capture men's minds or harness their opinions, but to bear witness continually, in his own work, that there is such a thing as singleness of mind or purity of heart, and that within the misery and squalor and stupidity of the modern world it is still possible to see God.

An artist who takes this view of his place in the world asks for independence, not that he may be proud before men, but that he may be quiet, and listen to his voices, and learn to speak a little of what they speak to him. He asks to be left alone that he may contemplate the mystery of life itself and bear witness to it.

To demand of artists that they enlist in the army of a particular ideology, however virtuous that ideology may be, is to demand of them something that is contrary to their nature. It is only the madness of collectivism that demands it, and everywhere in the world collectivism is dying. It is ceasing even to be fashionable. And just as it is beginning to be understood, in the sphere of economics, that only a free economy can save mankind from despair and that the State should impose no restraints upon a free economy except those which are necessary to prevent one man from tyrannizing over another, so it is beginning to be understood also that there should be no restraint upon artists unless they abuse their art libellously or seditiously. Those who were called 'modern' a few years ago, and are still talking of the movement of 'modern' thought towards a collective tyranny, have become old-fashioned without knowing it. If they can be withheld from conquering the world by force, Europe may advance towards a Re-enlightenment comparable with the Renaissance, and of such a Re-enlightenment the independence of artists is a condition.

To preserve and develop it is among the greatest needs of our time. For the moment it is hard. It is hard because totalitarians are deeply entrenched among us. It is harder because so many men of goodwill, Socialists, Liberals, even Conservatives, desiring social justice, are still prepared to play the collective game. The world is still maddened by

D

that collective vice which the Germans call *Angst* and which the apostles of materialistic Existentialism have exalted into a kind of virtue or necessity. From this the world has yet to free itself and the way to freedom lies through the demobilization of art so that it may no longer be called 'escapism' or 'treason by avoidance' to write Mozart's Quintet in G minor or Chopin's Third Étude.

We who write must play our part fearlessly. We must have the courage to consider the lilies, how they grow, so that the eye of our vision may be single. We must learn how to be still and without *Angst*, and the world must demand of us, not the mean and cowardly service of enlisting our minds in its regiments, but the supreme service of discovering that peace which passes understanding. The only contemptible 'escapism' is escape *into* the mass. The supreme cowardice is to run away from the responsibility of being an individual and unique creature, a child of God, and to take refuge in the anonymity of the crowd. The crowd is a word, not a reality. There is no reality except in the Spirit. Philosophically speaking, there is no such thing as The People. There is no such thing as Party. There is no such thing as Class. These things exist, but they have no being; they are not realities. When we go about in the world and look at men and women, we are not looking at 'The People'; we are not looking at a Nationality or a Class. We are looking at spirits inhabiting bodies, some darkened and imprisoned, some shining through the flesh; it is with them, and with their manifestation in nature, that art is concerned. Allow an artist to be about his business. He will march to no man's drum. He cannot enlist without betrayal, for, if he is an artist at all, he was enlisted long ago under another captain, not of this world.

# THE WORD 'SERENITY'

At the heart of the unease of the world as it moves on into the second half of the twentieth century is our sense that the tragedy in which we live is, as tragedy, bad. It is as though *Phèdre* were being written by a garage-boy or *Antony and Cleopatra* by an idiot. The lines do not scan, the structure is confused, no form is felt to be completing itself. The purgative effect of tragedy is absent.

One of the reasons is that, in each man's mind, events have become more and more widely separated from his sense of personal responsibility. Good and evil befall him like thunderbolts from the sky. He works hard, he prospers in his trade or profession, he saves money, he looks forward to independence in the future or to a holiday now, and suddenly one morning he awakes to find that a new series of arbitrary controls or a manipulation of the currency has ruined him. The explanations offered are jargon in his ears. He does not understand them and gravely suspects that the so-called 'experts', who contradict one another and whose prophecies are continually falsified, understand them little better than he. Of one thing only is he certain: that what has happened has happened independently of his conscious will. He is visited by a sense of the irrational, the arbitrary and the formless in human affairs. He begins to feel like a wasp trapped in a jam-jar half-filled with beer and honey. He has begun to climb out of the trap, to scale the glassy wall through

43

which he can see sunshine and freedom, when suddenly someone picks up the jar and swirls it round; he is thrown back into the trap again.

A second reason for the conversion of the human drama from high tragedy to a species of irrational farce is that it is continually interrupted and dominated by teams of clowns and robots, committees, councils, assemblies, conferences, societies, who run about the stage in criss-cross patterns, shouting in all the tongues of Babel that they have come to save the world and issuing communiqués elaborately designed to conceal meaning.

They carry initials on their backs. Something called, for example, the People's Consultative Council for the Prefabrication of Happiness becomes the P.C.C.P.H. These initials then begin to appear in the popular newspapers. 'The P.C.C.P.H., in consultation with the P.Q.R.S.T., decided yesterday that, in the cause of equality, all tall boys should have their feet cut off, but in deference to representations from the International Confederation of Shoemakers, the proposal has been referred to the approaching conference of R.S.T.U.' The father of a family, as he reads his newspaper, has long ago forgotten, if he ever knew, the meaning of these initials. They are placards carried on the backs of manikins who, in solemn confusion, skip across the stage of life; they are the cipher in which is written the farce that no one understands. Tragedy has lost its purgative power because it has no longer any lucidity. Life has become a screaming and a buzzing in the ears.

This is the appearance of things, not the reality. The Eumenides are still pursuing men and for the ancient reasons. The grace of God is still available to our undeserving. Our task is to re-establish in our minds the form and lucidity of the human drama. At present we are mistaking the nature of our problem. It is not at root a problem of activity, of running about the stage shouting that we know (or do not know) how the play should be rewritten; it is, on the contrary, a problem of stillness, of learning how to be still, how to listen, how to accept the human drama as a form which is completing itself and not as a whirling of incoherent fragments. We are still living, as mankind has always lived, in a tragedy which, like the tragedy of *Oedipus Coloneus*, has a solution; we are not living in a non-stop revue. To become incapable of making this distinction is to fall into the impiety of madness and despair.

• • • •

It is, then, perhaps desirable that, while politicians, economists and sociologists endeavour to force the play into the mould of their convictions, private men and women should approach it less violently and in a spirit of meditation. There is enough shouting; let us not increase it. There are enough infallible remedies; let us not add to them. Let us not attempt to re-write the drama of life, for we did not create life and do not know of how many acts the drama consists. Let us instead examine certain words which, even in our own lifetime, have lost or changed their meanings, and ask what is the significance of the loss or the change. In this way it may be possible to establish certain points of reference, a kind of Rosetta Stone, which shall make the contemporary tragedy decipherable by patient students.

• • • •

The words *serene* and *serenity* have almost vanished, and yet the idea they express has not ceased to exist. Why, then, have they vanished? Words are driven out of currency by our self-conscious avoidance of them. Fifty years ago our fathers and mothers would pursue elaborate circumlocutions, which we now smile at, in order to avoid words descriptive of parts of the body or functions of the body. Many of these words are now used freely, and we pride ourselves upon our emancipation. And yet it is to be remarked that there are other words which we avoid. If our parents were embarrassed by the things of the body, we are embarrassed by the things of the spirit.

Two striking instances occur in Mr. Somerset Maugham's recently published volume, *A Writer's Notebook*. He speaks of the danger of note-taking. It may, he says, cause an imaginative writer to lose the even and natural flow of his writing 'which comes from allowing the unconscious that full activity which is *somewhat pompously* known as inspiration'. (The italics are mine.) Later in the same book, he quotes Pascal: 'Mais quand l'univers l'écraseroit, l'homme seroit encore plus noble que ce qui le tue, parce qu'il meurt; et l'avantage que l'univers a sur lui, l'univers n'en sait rien. Toute notre dignité consiste donc en la pensée.' And Mr. Somerset Maugham adds: 'I think there is some disparagement today in the notion of dignity, and I believe that the French word is better translated into English by the word nobility.'

These two passages are deeply significant. Mr. Maugham is one of the most distinguished and the most popular of living dramatists. He is a shrewd and accurate observer of the fashionable habits of the contemporary mind. If he cannot use the word 'inspiration' without apologizing for it as being 'somewhat pompous' and if he says that today the notion of dignity is disparaging, then we may be sure that 'dignity' and 'inspiration' are among the words that modern men avoid as their parents avoided, in embarrassment, the words concerned with excretion. Why? Because, like our parents, we are ashamed. But we are differently ashamed. Why are we ashamed of the great words of the spirit — dignity, inspiration, liberty, serenity? Because the ideas within these words have been too often abused for us to abuse them. They record our failures. They pronounce our doom. No one is eager to echo the words of his own sentence of death.

Again, this is the appearance of things, not the reality. Dignity, inspiration, liberty, serenity are not the words of a death-sentence. Only the insane disorder of our stage, the corruption of the human tragedy by the wild unreason of farce, makes us reject our own means of salvation — that is to say, the solution of tragedy which proceeds from completion of its form. To say that inspiration is 'pompous' and that the word 'dignity' has a meaning of disparagement is to let loose a troupe of clowns to slap Phèdre with their balloons and drag Cleopatra from her monument. This, precisely, is what we have done, this is the degree of decivilization to which we have attained; but if we are so arrogant as to suppose that our clowns will prevail, we deceive ourselves. A gust of wind will blow them from the stage. They will be terribly silenced. The human tragedy will become lucid again.

. . . . .

Lucid. Serene is the greater word, for serenity includes the idea of lucidity. A serene sky is both calm and clear, but in a stormy sky there may be lucid intervals. Nevertheless it is important to associate the two words, for penetration by light is the essence of serenity. It is possible to be calm without being serene: a face may be dully or stupidly calm, but a serene face is one through which the light of the spirit shines.

As the word serenity appears and reappears in my thought like the face of an angel looking in through a window that I can seldom open, I am visited by the remembrance of two works of art of which I have often written in my novels, and now, as I write this, I seem to understand them anew, or, rather, I would say, to receive them anew. They are 'The Agony in the Garden' by Giovanni Bellini in the National Gallery in London, and the tomb of Ilaria del Carretto by Jacopo della Quercia in the cathedral at Lucca. The Bellini has been moved. Formerly there was a bench directly opposite it on which one might sit and watch. At first it was a cause of distress in me that, as I sat, my line of vision was constantly interrupted by other visitors to the gallery who passed between the picture and me, but gradually I became accustomed to this and began even to have profit in it, for to lose the picture thus and to find it again, constantly and serenely glowing, unchanged by the eclipse of my having been blinded to it, was to be made aware of it as an emblem of Grace. Now it has been moved. I must stand before it, an island in the stream of human bodies, and to this I have not yet so disciplined myself that I am undisturbed by it. But by this disturbance, this weakness of self-discipline, I am not alienated from this picture as I might be from another as beautiful but different in kind. The Bellini will wait, like an absolution, until I am able to receive it again.

Ilaria meanwhile waits in Lucca. She is calm and, at the same time, an embodiment of the distinction between calmness and serenity. What is that distinction? However we attempt to define it, the idea of light enters into our definition. From Ilaria there shines an interior radiance such as exists, within my knowledge, nowhere else in sculpture, the same radiance as glows, about the head of the kneeling Jesus, in Bellini's Italian sky — a sky so profoundly serene that Bellini, who has given a halo to each of the sleeping disciples, has given none to their Master; the sky itself being, of His holiness, a sufficient emblem.

Now, it is remarkable that of these two masterpieces, so triumphantly serene, one is a figure of a young woman dead – 'L'homme seroit encore plus noble que ce qui le tue, parce qu'il meurt'; and the other, a picture of the garden of Gethsemane, marks a supreme point in the Christian tragedy, beyond which, in the Christian view, lies neither despair nor chaos nor any destructive finality, but that 'solution' of the human tragedy which, in the Christian context, is called redemption and is precisely analogous to the Greek tragedians' idea of expiatory release.

It seems, then, that serenity is among the essential distinctions between great tragedy and corrupt melodrama or farce; between form and formlessness. I dare to add that serenity marks an essential distinction between good and evil, and that its presence or its absence is one of the means by which good and evil may be defined. The alternative is not, as modern criticism of life and of art often pretends, between optimism and pessimism, between sentimentality and objectively observed fact, between romanticism and naturalism. These distinctions, though perhaps useful for the purposes of classification, are not essential. The essential distinction is between the serene or light-admitting and the unserene or light-excluding. No more profoundly tragic music has ever been written than the slow movement of Mozart's Quintet in G Minor, and none more serene. It has the quality of Bellini's sky and of Ilaria's sleep.

.    .    .    .

Therefore . . .

.    .    .    .

Ah! but there are too many 'therefores'! I wish to compel no one to an opinion . . . Have you ever watched a child, in the full activity of childhood, halt as though an invisible hand had touched his shoulder, and stare? I remember such occasions in my own childhood, and in my manhood also, when a thing seen, which a moment ago was one of many and of no particular significance, has become singular, has separated itself from the stream of consciousness, and has become not an object but a source. What is the child staring at? Not at the flower or the drop of water or the face. The thing seen, which ordinarily halts our observation, has become not a wall but a window. The opaque has become the serene; he is looking through it, through the disparate appearances of life, which we falsely call reality, towards the origin of that light by which all things are seen. What awes the child is not that he has arrived at an intellectual understanding of the order of things but that he has perceived that there is an order of things.

Is it not the purpose of art to renew this perception? To record facts is journalism; to comment upon them is still journalism; to arrange them in an order convenient to an ideology is to lie; to penetrate them is to be an artist. An artist is a child who stares, not at the imprisoning walls of life, but outward through the window. Degas said somewhere that he looked through keyholes; I think he looked outward. *Là tout n'est qu'ordre et beauté.*

But an artist is more than a child who stares and sees. He must communicate his vision. His own work must itself be serene — that is to say, not opaque, not obscure, but penetrable and penetrated by light. This, one might be tempted to say at first, is an effect obtainable by intellectual lucidity, but it is untrue; the Code Napoléon is intellectually lucid, but, valuable though it may have been to Stendhal, it is not in itself a work of art. The effect of art is an interaction between the artist and his audience. It is necessary, therefore, that he shall say clearly what he has to say and *at the same time* induce in his audience a condition of mind in which they are capable of receiving what he has said and what — because language is imperfect — he has been unable to express intellectually. If he is to communicate his total vision, he must communicate his spell as well as his thought.

Rhyme, rhythm, scansion, structure — all those things which are comprehended in the idea of form — are not decorations or pedantic rules but a means of casting that spell without which the communications of art are necessarily incomplete. Their value lies in this fact: that they create in the listener a series of expectations which are continually fulfilled and so make him receptive of that idea of '*ordre et beauté*' which seems to be contradicted by the outward appearances of things. When once this receptive condition has been induced in him, he becomes capable of reading between the lines of intellectual language. The sky of tragedy becomes, for him, serene.

·     ·     ·

The human tragedy, as it now appears, has become farcical, brutal and incoherent because in it neither intellectual lucidity nor the creation of form is pursued. One may understand perfectly why men are going mad if one imagines what would have happened if Shakespeare had written in a secret code or Racine in contempt of the alexandrine, and the world had been compelled to listen to the result on loud-speakers all day and all night. The confessions, contrary to nature and reason, which are regularly made at Soviet trials are presumably obtained by the application of such mental torments, and there are plays and poetry and music being written and pictures being painted in Western Europe which are confusions in the same kind. They have neither intellectual lucidity nor form. They utter but do not communicate. The human child, looking at them, sees only hideous walls which shout at him and close in upon him.

May it not be the supreme gift of France to Western civilization that she restore order and serenity to the human tragedy? Someone must draw again in the tradition of Ingres. I did not say 'like Ingres'; I said 'in the tradition of Ingres' as one might have said of Ingres himself that he drew 'in the tradition' of Raphael. The question is not whether the human figure is idealized or un-idealized. The question is whether it stands on its feet.

May it not be the supreme gift of those who speak the language of Shakespeare that they restore vision and serenity to the human tragedy? It is not to be forgotten that the serenest of plays was called *The Tempest*. Nor is it to be forgotten, while we are thinking of Ingres and Bellini in our search for the vital link between form and serenity, that it was not an Academician but Renoir who wrote:

Mais, si le métier est la base et la solidité de l'art, il n'est pas tout. Il y a autre chose, dans l'art des anciens, qui rend leurs productions si belles: c'est cette sérénité qui fait qu'on ne se lasse pas de

les voir, et qui nous donne l'idée de l'oeuvre éternelle. Cette
sérénité, ils l'avaient en eux, non pas seulement par l'effet de leur
vie simple et tranquille, mais encore grâce à leur foi religieuse.
Ils avaient conscience de leur faiblesse, et, dans leurs succès
comme dans leurs revers, ils associaient la divinité à leurs actes.
Dieu est toujours là, et l'homme ne compte pas. Chez les Grecs,
c'était Apollon ou Minerve; les peintres de l'époque de Giotto
prenaient aussi un protecteur céleste. C'est ainsi que leurs
oeuvres acquéraient cet aspect de douce sérénité qui leur donne
ce charme profond et les rend immortelles.

But, if craftsmanship is the foundation and the strength of art,
it is not all. There is something else, in the art of our forefathers,
which makes their productions so beautiful: it is that serenity
which causes one never to tire of looking at them and makes
upon us an impression of timelessness. This serenity they had in
them, not only as an effect of their simple and tranquil life, but
thanks also to their religious faith. They were aware of their own
failings, and, in their success as in their reverses, they saw the
hand of God. God is always there and man does not count. With
the Greeks, it was Apollo or Minerva; and the painters of Giotto's
time also looked to heavenly protection. So it was that their
works took on that sweet serenity which gives them their profound charm and makes them immortal.

Nothing is so certain as that, in the present condition of
the world, there can be no deeper betrayal of civilization
than to blur meaning, and, in art, to substitute chaos for
form. The betrayal is committed, in nine cases out of ten,
as an excuse for incompetence; the draughtsman who cannot
compose breaks his picture into disordered fragments, as
one who is losing at chess might overthrow the board; but
sometimes the betrayal is deliberate so that serenity may be
banished from the earth and the forces of evil dictate to the
inhabitants of a snake-pit.

·     ·     ·     ·     ·

Now let us consider other great words that are sick. 'Order', for example. Why has it become dissociated from 'Liberty'? Or 'Beauty'. By the conspiracy of what gutter-snipes has it been drawn into contempt? ... But that, as Alfred de Vigny wrote so often in his Journal, is a *poème à faire....*

# THE WORD 'ACADEMIC'

THERE are words which stand in need of rescue — such words as *serene*, or *pure*, or *prevent*, whose older meanings are being trodden down by their newer. No one in his senses wishes to restrict the growth of language, and it is part of the genius of English, a reason for the incomparable richness of its poetic overtones, that it is so malleable, and so easily allows the adjectival use of nouns and the addition of new meanings to old words. But the gain is cancelled out if the new meaning destroys or, even worse, corrupts the old. There was a time — and the practice, for all we know, may continue — in which schoolmasters and schoolmistresses would teach their pupils that, in the Beatitude 'Blessed are the pure in heart', the word *pure* was directed to the idea of sexual morality. The dictionary gives this meaning to the word very far down the column, and even quotes the Beatitude as an example of a different meaning. Nevertheless, the notion that *pure* is an equivalent of *chaste* has steadily gained ground. Even where other meanings survive they have been weakened. The phrase *pure nonsense* no longer, in the popular mind, means what it should mean, namely: *nonsense unmixed with anything else*. It has acquired a pejorative sense, and if I were to say: 'The greatness of Wilde's *The Importance of Being Earnest*, and its distinction from his other plays, consists in its being pure nonsense,' I should by many be misunderstood and suspected of having contradicted myself. The idea that, in the Gospel, purity of heart means, not chastity, but a more profound spiritual singleness and incorruption has been darkened in the contemporary mind by the shadow which the sexual meaning of *pure* has cast upon its older meanings.

Against this overshadowing of valuable words we are bound to fight if we would preserve lucidity of thought. Certain words, *democracy* for example, have been so misused that they appear to be lost; only a very long holiday can restore them. But other threatened words are still worth fighting for, and *academic* is among them.

The last meaning given by the dictionary is usurping the places of all others. The Shorter Oxford, 1947, says:

1. Of the school or philosophy of Plato; sceptical 1610.
2. Of or belonging to an academy: collegiate, scholarly 1588.
3. Of or belonging to a learned society; belonging to an Academician 1879.
4. Not leading to a decision; unpractical (*mod.*).

The fourth meaning is, as it stands, unpleasant enough, but the lexicographers have been, I think, too gentle. In popular speech the word *academic* has become, or is fast becoming, opprobrious. An 'academic discussion' is ordinarily thought of as being a discussion which not only arrives at no conclusion but is to be contemned for that reason; it does not occur to the untrained mind that an inconclusive discussion may be in itself valuable. The arrogance of the half-educated can, in the conditions of the modern world, be abruptly overbearing, and it is in the nature of this arrogance to refuse to acknowledge that there are unanswerable questions which are nevertheless worth asking. To ask such questions, to discuss them, to observe how many other questions are implicit in all the answers, or seeming answers, that thought may supply, and to be led by this process into an understanding that knowledge can lead us only into the foothills of wisdom, is to be in the strictest sense — that is to say, in the Socratic sense — 'academic'. The modern, popular mind will have none of this; it is, in Meredith's phrase, 'hot for certainties', and feels that any discussion which does not attain to certainty is a waste of time, 'unpractical', 'academic'. The effect of thinking in this way is to make the thinker infinitely gullible. So impatient is he of the refinements, the reservations, the nice distinctions inherent in any argument which makes, or strives to make, a genuine approach to truth, so eager is he to be 'practical', to arrive, to 'have something to bite on', that he falls an easy victim to crude, assertive, emotional propaganda. Because it has always been a prime duty of great 'academies' to fortify their members against this form of surrender, a feeling of hostility to the academic idea has arisen in the popular mind. This is not contradicted by the steadily increasing demand for entry into universities, for the demand is accompanied by another: that the universities themselves be 'popularized', that they approach more and more nearly to the condition of vocational training-colleges, that they become more 'practical', less 'academic'. The word *university* has not become opprobrious; it has been saved by its association with popular notions of utility; while the word *academic* has had heaped upon it the dark meanings of priggish, futile, unpractical, anti-social.

Changes in a language reflect changes in the needs and habits of a people; they are, therefore, part of the material of social historians. Among such material the changed meaning

E

of *academic* is of importance, as the changed meaning of *prevent* is not. It is important because it represents a recently changed attitude of mind. It seems to be true that when we begin to dislike or fear an idea which formerly we admired, our commonest method of self-protection is to overlay with scornful meanings the words attached to those ideas. This applies to *aristocratic* and even *gentleman* and *lady*. Nowadays *young lady* means commonly a shop-assistant, and the still uncorrupted word *gentlewoman* has had to be revived to carry the meaning of gentle birth and upbringing. But here a distinction has to be made. The word *academic* stands in a class apart — apart even from *Academy*.

The dislike which has given an envious, and sometimes even a contemptuous, meaning to *aristocracy* is kindred to the dislike which now darkens the word *Academy*; it is a dislike of exclusiveness, of closed societies, of the privileged few; it is an old dislike which, though it takes different forms in different ages, springs not from envy alone but from a healthy suspicion of closed doors. Except when the guillotine begins to rattle, there is good-humour in it and a lingering respect. In England, the word *Academy* ordinarily means the Royal Academy; in France, it suggests the five academies which compose the Institut de France, and, in particular, the oldest of these, l'Académie Française. Certainly, it is a popular habit to laugh at the forty *immortels* who sit in the Académie Française, to emphasize the demerits of some of them, to leave unmentioned the giants who have been of its number, and to chuckle over the recollection of the great men whom it has excluded. Yet those Frenchmen who, knowing that they would be elected, have refused to stand must be few indeed. The Royal Academy enjoys less prestige largely because it makes itself responsible, as l'Académie

Française does not, for a huge public exhibition of work much of which is necessarily below the standard of its own academicians; but it enjoys prestige in the same kind. Young painters sometimes rebel against it for a time, but, if they can, they come in in the end. 'The Academy' in London and in Paris is an object of satire, but of satire which is an expression of human nature itself and implies an underlying respect.

The emotion attached to the popular use of the adjective *academic* is different in kind; it is by no means good-humoured, it is extremely modern and it represents a new hostility to a set of ideas hitherto held in honour. This hostility is directed against individual excellence in craftsmanship based upon long apprenticeship and a study of the masters. At one time, in the world of painters and draughtsmen, the word was descriptive, saying of a picture only that it was in a particular style, without praising or condemning that style; later, it suggested in the picture so described a certain formality which the speaker was inclined to regard as excessive; but today the word is seldom used of a picture except in a tone which suggests that because the picture displays a studied craftsmanship it is, therefore, lifeless, opposed to the spirit of the age, and contemptible. The same is true of writing; it is considered a virtue in a poet not to scan or punctuate, and in an actor to deliver even classical verse, which does scan, as if it did not. Outside the world of art the same prejudice exists. A Judge who gives a judgement which is an accurate rendering of the law but is opposed nevertheless to popular sentiment will be attacked, not openly because he has released a prisoner whom his critic would have liked to condemn, but on the ground that his judgement, 'though it may have been right in law', was pedantic, legalistic, too reliant upon authority, 'academic'. The time may not be far off when a plumber who knows his job and so arouses an uncomfortable sense of inequality and inferiority in men who have scamped their apprenticeship will be described as an 'academic' plumber. The word has become a synonym for *unpractical*, as the dictionary says, but the dictionary has not remarked to how great an extent whatever is accurate, precise, finely worked, whatever is the product of care, of patience, of time, whatever bespeaks an inequality of learning or talent, has come to be considered unpractical and so 'academic'. How long will it be before there is a demand for the abolition of Class Lists in universities?

But there is a little hope. There are signs that the tide is turning. In France, soon after the death of Anatole France, it was as much as one's life was worth to speak in praise of him. Now the genuinely young men are returning to his work. The same is true of Musset and, in music, of Chopin. In England, Tennyson is being restored to his place; even his mastery of verse is being seen, not as an 'academic' defect, but as a virtue to be studied. Turgenev, as I have not ceased to foretell for the last twenty years, is returning; his novels are being everywhere re-issued and a new translation of *First Love* by Isaiah Berlin has set a new academic *cachet* on the old master. Next, it may be Landor's turn. A revival of verses that may be scanned, of sentences that may be analysed, perhaps even of plumbing that works, will give us an opportunity, in our praise of these achievements, to resist the decay of the word *academic*. Our case rests upon the truth that it is not, in an artist, a crime against democracy to have learned how to draw, or, in a university, an insult to a young man 'hot for certainties' to teach him how to think.

# OF LIVING IN THE PRESENT

To live in the present does not imply rashness or irresponsibility or selfishness; it is not an act of hedonism or of cowardly escape. It is to live with instant appreciation of the good in life and in freedom from obsessive anxiety. 'Take no thought for the morrow' has never been a command against imagining the future. It is a command against the corroding anxieties which, like acid or rust, eat away our life and our confidence in it.

There are fashions in anxiety as there are in all else. The most dangerous of modern anxieties is collective — a sense, which some have, that they are passengers in a runaway tramcar which is carrying them so fast and so uncontrollably into an abyss that to look at the view has become meaningless. To this anxiety of Collective Disaster we give many names — war, atomism, communism, slump, and even, if we are fashionable intellectuals, existentialism — but under any name it has the same effect. It is a negation of the present. It takes the taste out of life. It makes an absurdity of faith, and of love an excretion.

In Shakespeare's day — or, shall we say rather, during the hundred or more years that had their centre in the year 1600 — the over-riding human obsession was the brevity of human life. It had always been a preoccupation, and the Renaissance drove it to a climax. Life had become so exciting, so sweetly dangerous, so full of brilliant speculation and untold possibility, that men could not bear to be parted from it. Gradually the intensity of this rebellion against time faded and the passionate lyricism of Shakespeare's

> Then come kiss me, sweet and twenty!
> Youth's a stuff will not endure,

became the decorative charm of Herrick's

> Gather ye rosebuds while ye may,
> Old Time is still a-flying:
> And this same flower that smiles today
> Tomorrow will be dying.

But the theme of both poets — a dominant theme of poetry in all ages but our own — was life's brevity: a theme which drove some to look for the consolations of another life and others to seek, as Shakespeare and Herrick did in the lines quoted and as the great pagans did continually, an intensification of the living instant.

. . . .

In us, all this is changed. The modern attitude is not of protest against the brevity of life but of complaint against its sickness. Witness T. S. Eliot's two most famous lines:

> This is the way the world ends
> Not with a bang but a whimper.

The predominant note is of futility and vertigo. Ours is not an age of faith; our poets, for the most part, have lost the power to offer, and our mechanized millions have lost the power to accept, a promise of another world either as compensation for the suffering of this or as fulfilment of its experience. Nor have we any longer that overflowing glory in life here which the Elizabethans had — a glory of which the tragic splendour of *Romeo and Juliet* or even the lightning-

shot blackness of *The Duchess of Malfi* is as much a proof
as the radiance of *As You Like It*. How these men glowed,
even in their despairs! Their hells at least flamed; ours sizzle
like an electric fire during a power-cut. Who doubts that,
even in the torment of *Lear* and the agony of the Sonnets,
Shakespeare was filled with a sense of the glory of touching,
of tasting, of smelling, hearing and seeing — of suffering
also; the plain glory of being alive? Not until *The Tempest*
did a deep shadow fall upon that glory of his, and he begin to
withdraw deliberately into other worlds than this.

We do not share his passion for the hour. Many of our
poets and painters and dramatists, if they adhere to the
fashion of disintegration and non-lucidity which is expressed
by Sartre and Picasso, teach that life is formless and without
seizable significance. They are no longer rebellious against
the gods as Prometheus was, for they acknowledge no gods,
and in their eyes to rebel is as much a form of sentimentality
as to accept. They are no longer constructively critical even
of man, for they do not acknowledge individual responsibility. They can hate, but not love, for hatred is sterile and
consistent with their doctrine of race-suicide, whereas love
claims to be fertile and is, in their view, falsely romantic.
The kisses of Sweet-and-Twenty are for them not an innocent glory but a guilty lie. Living themselves in a disease of
guilt and anxiety, they have found that the disease is contagious. They have trodden down the undiseased poets of
our age — De la Mare, Brooke, Nichols, Flecker, and Andrew Young. Andrew Young is a parson now living in England. His rank is with Vaughan, Crashaw and Traherne. But
he is undiseased. How many readers have been allowed to
hear of him?

From this disease — this repudiation of the reason, the

beauty, the order and even the sadness of life — we have to liberate ourselves. The alternative is world-madness under the pressure of obsessive anxieties. We have to learn again how to conjugate our lives in the present tense. 'I am, thou art . . .' which was Shakespeare's answer to the fear of death, may still be our answer to those who now deny any meaning in life.

.     .     .     .

If we would learn anew how to live in the present, we must ask what the present is. Is it this year, this month, this day, this hour? It is none of these. It is a point in time which, like a point in mathematics, has position but no magnitude. It is — and instantly it was. It was the present and is become the past; and we have plunged on in pursuit of that limitless future which, like a ghost that we cannot touch, is forever receding before us.

If this were not true, if we had power to arrest the present and dwell in it, there would be no poetry and no religion, for both poetry and religion are the outcome of a conflict in the human mind between a desire to catch time by the hair, to arrest the fugitive instant, and a sense that this is impossible. When we have grasped that all experience is made up, not of years or hours or minutes, but of infinite smallnesses without duration — in brief, that it is an absolute continuity — then and then only has eternity a meaning for us. Neither the infinitely small nor the infinitely great is comprehensible while we think in terms of clocks, but both become imaginable when we accept the radical truth that clocks are unreal.

It follows that to think of ourselves as 'moderns' is to think of ourselves falsely, for the idea of modernism is the idea of ourselves marching at the head of a column, whereas, in truth, each instant of our experience is timeless, and the notion of a column or even of a stream is illusory. No one has ever said this clearly because our language will not permit it to be said clearly; our language, and all its images, depend upon approximate measurements of time and space. We speak of minutes, of seconds, of fractions of a second, and all the fractions are too large to express timelessness. We speak of years, of centuries, of eras, and all the eras are too small. When the poet Blake spoke of seeing a world in a grain of sand and eternity in an hour, the grain of sand and the hour were his approximations to truth, and poetry itself can go no farther. The present and eternity are the same; both are beyond the reach of measurement and of words.

.    .    .    .

It would seem then that the first thing required of a man who wishes to learn again how to live in the present is to grasp that, when he has succeeded in doing so, he will have succeeded also in living in the light of eternity. He will be an inhabitant of the infinitely great as well as of the infinitely small. He will see in each of his acts not the futility which all our endeavours and all our delights seem to have when the clock scorns and belittles them, but the value which they all have (for good or for evil) when they are seen in the aspect of timelessness.

These things are best understood in concrete and perhaps trivial instances. Look at the photograph of a woman in a dress and hat fashionable ten years ago. The dress and the hat which she (and you and I) then thought beautiful now appear ridiculous and perhaps even grotesque. Are they for that reason necessarily grotesque and ridiculous? Or do they appear so only because they are seen with the prejudice of our own modernism, in our enslavement to the clock? Look at a portrait of the same woman in the same dress and hat painted by a great artist ten years ago — will that seem absurd as the photograph did? Almost certainly not, for art presents all its subjects 'in the aspect of timelessness' as photography does not. Or look at the photograph itself when it is not ten but a hundred years old — do you suppose that the hat and the dress will appear grotesque as they do now?

All our acts, all our thoughts, like our dresses and hats, are distorted and falsified if we see them with the eyes of a clock. Their value appears only if they are seen timelessly. Then and then only is their beauty or their ugliness seen independently of their fashion. Then only is innocence seen through guilt, and pardon through sin, and safety through fear, and life through death.

.    .    .    .

We arrive then at a conclusion, which may seem at first a heresy to certain men and women anxious to prove themselves good citizens, that the difficulty of Western man in freeing himself from obsessive anxieties is not, as is often supposed, a result of the virtue and sensitiveness of his social conscience but springs from his misuse of it. The misuse consists in his failure to grasp that to think of anything and judge anything (even oneself) in terms of defeatism is to think of it wrongly and to judge it falsely. The falseness is not made less by an attempt to disguise defeatism under different names which have a fashionable sound — such names as 'modernism' and sometimes 'existentialism'.

This is a difficult subject and I do not wish to discuss here the differences, which are profound, between the Christian and integrating existentialism of Kierkegaard and Gabriel

Marcel, and the materialistic and disintegrating existentialism of Sartre. My point is that the very word 'existentialism'
has become a smart, pseudo-intellectual badge worn by people
who are not philosophers at all but who have lost the poise
and moral courage which enable men to live in the present
without panic. To live in the present is to live sanely and
gratefully. To repudiate the present, to treat it as an exist-
entialist dust-storm, to gnash our teeth and shrug our
shoulders and say of all experience 'it couldn't matter less'
is to exist neurotically.

It is precisely in their rejection of this kind of false intellectualism that the people of the United States might become, and perhaps are now becoming, leaders of a genuinely
new development of world-thought. Their social conscience
is not opposed to their individualism but is rooted in it, and
although they, in common with all the world, are menaced
by the habit of group-thinking, they have an inherent
strength to resist the slavery of collectivism. One of the chief
evidences of this resistance is each man and woman's power
to face honestly the difficulties and dangers of the contemporary world without ceasing to be able to live in the present and taste it and rejoice in it. The more dangerous the
world appears to be, the more invulnerable must our individualism be made. We have to hold fast to the natural
good of our personal lives — the pleasures of family and
friendship, of art and nature, of memory and of fresh experience — pleasures which depend upon the liveliness of
our individual response to them. To allow that response to
be blunted, or to be ashamed of it because some call it
'romantic', is to make dust and ashes of our life here. We
have therefore to reject as false the poems, the plays and the
novels which preach the doctrines of futility and violence;

we have to observe, quite fearlessly, that, when they seem to be attacking the present only, they are in fact attacking life itself.

I saw a French play not long ago, written with delicacy and power, of which the argument was that, in present conditions, the love of a young man and woman must inevitably decay and that it could be saved from corruption only if, in the full tide of their love, they went out and hanged themselves. That this extreme despondency is representative of modern thought I do not suggest, but it does mark an intellectual tendency which has, I believe, arisen from a moral cowardice masquerading as anti-romantic realism. Thomas Hardy was not an optimist but he came much nearer to the truth of our relationship to the tragedies of history when he wrote:

> Yonder a maid and her wight
> Come whispering by:
> War's annals will cloud into night
> Ere their story die.

It is necessary that the world learn again to conjugate the verb to be. 'I am, thou art, He is' is the sanity of love and faith, and the atom bomb does not affect it.

# TIME OUT

*Release from the Pressure of Existence is a Means of Progress*

TIME Out is altogether different from a holiday — a rarer and more valuable experience. It is a period, perhaps of a year or more, perhaps of only a few weeks, in which our whole existence is different from our customary existence. Living for the time being in a new world, we are released from the pressures and responsibilities of the old. The change may not at first be welcome; we may even resist it and complain about it; it may, as Robinson Crusoe found, plunge us into labours and anxieties greater than those we have left behind. Nevertheless if no brackets ever appear in a man's life, he becomes a creature of routine and loses the power to renew himself; and this is a danger which is threatening the health and happiness of our civilization.

. . . . .

I remember well, and always with pleasure, the opportunities that I myself have had to see the little drama of my own life suddenly transferred to a new stage with a new cast.

In the year 1913, I was a very young naval officer in the China Seas. Wishing to be a writer, I applied for permission to leave the Navy, which was granted. I travelled home across Siberia, and found myself in England as a civilian.

This in itself was an adventure, for I had worn uniform and lived under a strict discipline since I was twelve.

Soon afterwards, I went into deep country, lodged with an old tutor in a farm, and set about learning enough Latin and Greek to enable me to go to Oxford. To others this may sound commonplace enough; to me, because my life's point of view had been changed, it was the bravest of new worlds. Scholarship was a dream; I pursued it with passionate ardour. The months I spent in that remote cottage, often working eighteen hours a day, were for me Time Out in the completest sense. During them I became a different human being.

My next Time Out was forced upon me and was at the outset exceedingly unwelcome. My labours had succeeded, examinations were passed, and during the summer of 1914 I waited with burning eagerness for my first term at Oxford to begin. All my mind was given up to the enchanting disciplines of poetry and prose. Suddenly, on the 4th of August, war broke out, and I was a naval officer again.

Not, alas, in a ship. The ships were full, the Fleet was at sea. I was attached, as an infantry officer, to the Naval Brigades which Mr. Churchill formed at that time and sent to the defence of Antwerp. The siege and the fall of Antwerp were, I suppose, Time Out also; they live in brackets in my mind and are not to be described here. Antwerp fell. For the greater part of the First Brigade, retreat to the coast was cut off. Within two months of the outbreak of war I was a prisoner. Early in 1915, at the time of my twenty-first birthday, my fellow-officers and I were walking round the ramparts of a moated fortress in Holland, not in the least knowing how long this interlude in our lives would be or how it would end or what use we should make of it.

Nearly all of us, I think, genuinely believed at first that we had suffered a misfortune. Even our friends in England took the same view, writing to offer their sympathy in our bad luck; and it is true that, for many officers, the period of imprisonment was a time of suffering. Some were still on the active list; for them, to be out of the battle, to miss the chance of distinction and promotion, was as infuriating as it had been for Nelson's Captain Troubridge to run the *Culloden* on to a shoal at the moment when his fellow-captains were sailing in to the Battle of the Nile. Others among my companions were airmen whose machines had been shot down, and upon airmen the stress of flying has often the effect of drug-taking — deny it to them and they lose their nerve or their temper, they are on edge and deeply unhappy.

But I was neither an airman nor any longer a naval officer with naval ambitions. Although at the beginning I was conventional enough to regret my imprisonment, the day came on which I saw it as an opportunity. I intrigued to escape, struggling to bribe servants within the fortress and to make clandestine arrangements outside it; I shared in the digging of a tunnel which, as I have told in my novel *The Fountain*, came to nothing. But these attempts to escape were a matter of duty. I began to love those wooded ramparts and the flat country stretching out beyond them and the long, peaceful, repetitive days and nights.

This was Time Out from the stress of ordinary existence and it came at the time when it is most valuable — at the very beginning of young manhood. Our ancestors were wise in decreeing that their young men, before they launched out into the business of life, should make The Grand Tour — a long and leisurely journey through Europe. Its value

was not only that it enabled them to see the world and
civilize themselves by contact with European society, but
that it took them away from home and from the too familiar
stresses, emotional and intellectual, which beset us when we
are twenty-one.

My walk round those ramparts was my Grand Tour and it
came when I needed it. I had not known that I needed it. I
had been eager to go to Oxford; the war had seemed a cruel
interruption, and by no means a blessing. But imprisonment
was a blessing. It gave me a chance, it even compelled me,
to sort out my values — to discover what I deeply cared for
in life, and why. All men and women need periodically that
chance, that compulsion, and under the continuous pressure
of modern life they get it too seldom. That, I believe, is why
our civilization, for all its scientific advance, has a tendency
to go stale. We snatch holidays, but they are very like our
ordinary life except that they are more expensive. We do not
take Time Out in which to renew ourselves — and the
world.

The delight of my imprisonment was that it gave me
freedom such as I had never known before. I am sometimes
told by the elderly that the young are 'carefree'; they must
either have forgotten their own youth or have been very dull
and unimaginative during that perilous time. Certainly I
had not been carefree as I looked forward to the University
and beyond. The Navy is not a rich but it is a secure profession; I had spent years in qualifying for it, and now, by
my own rash choice, had thrown security away. My father
had backed and would continue to back me, but I knew very
well how much my decision had cost him. At the moment
when I had been on the point of earning my own living by
the profession of the sea, I had elected to become an under-

graduate and to say, without hope of early proof, that some day I should earn my living by my pen. Ought I instead to become a barrister? Ought I to chose some solid, bread-and-butter profession to sustain me until the day came on which someone would pay to read what I wrote? I had been full of anxiety, I had been weighed down by a sense of responsibility for my own life, during that summer of 1914.

Now, in the fortress, immediate responsibility and the need for urgent decision were lifted from me. I had my pay, my food, my housing, and cost no one anything. I had no official duties, for we officers had been separated from our men. I could not, if I wanted to, take a job or go into a business or in any way worship Mammon. There was no Mammon to worship and there were no women to fall in love with.

The fates had suddenly given me Time Out — infinite time as far as I could tell. There were no telephones, and even letters were of the kind that did not have to be answered. No one kept an engagement-book, for there were no engagements; there was, in effect, no time. Until the moment should come in which the Germans decided to go home again, there were no calendars, even of the years. The French wars, in the days of Pitt and Nelson and Wellington, had lasted twenty years; these might last as long. Here was my opportunity to learn French, to read history, to think — not of today or tomorrow — but at long-term.

To be a prisoner with an indefinite sentence is not ordinarily considered a desirable fate, but if you are not of an impatient temperament it can be very like heaven.

. . . . .

This Time Out was thrust upon me and I take no credit except for having recognized and accepted it when it came.

F

Perhaps we can seldom do more than that. Holidays can be planned, but Times Out — the supreme recreative pauses in our lives — come to us, if they come at all, less as a consequence of a deliberate exercise of our own wills than as rewards of destiny. In another language, they are the gifts of God; but we have to learn how to value and accept them.

.    .    .    .

If a friend, having read what I have just written, were to ask: 'How can I have Time Out? How, under the pressures and responsibilities of my ordinary life, can I have opportunity for a recreative pause?' I could give him no answer that he would at once recognize as being valid in his own case. There can be no answer except: 'By desiring it, by imagining it, by not rebelling against it, by not hardening your heart.'

This applies to the condition of the whole world — to our politics, our economics, our education, our literature. We are obsessed by pathological anxiety and by a kind of active frenzy — a desperate and confused desire to 'do something' about we know not what. We should do better sometimes to stand aside, to meditate, to allow fresh ideas (which may be very old ideas not to be found on the agenda of any pressure-group) to flow into us.

In politics we are over-legislating and over-governing; the nations need quiet administration, continuity, rest. One does not obtain peace by agitating for it but by living it.

In economics, we are driving ourselves into a condition of incomprehensible artificiality because we are struggling to interfere too much, too often, and *at too short-term* with the natural laws of supply and demand. We are being poisoned by expedients as the body may be poisoned by potent medicines. The democracies of the world are voting for too much too soon. They are choking themselves, like greedy children.

In education, we are keeping too many people too long at school, and subjecting them to a rule based upon an assumption that is false at root: namely, that they are all equally able and willing to receive the same intellectual nourishment. So we are fostering in the young, who are fully aware of their differences of capacity, that profound anxiety, that sense of being enclosed by the irrational, the unnatural, the uncontrollable, which is the source of contemporary despairs. It is useless and positively evil to thrust a watered-down intellectualism upon those who, for better or for worse, are not intellectuals. To put it simply: some are manual workers, some are solitaries, some are poets, many are by nature religious. It is madness, and it begets world-madness, to educate them *en masse* in the ideal of sceptical and intellectual materialism.

In literature and in all the arts there is a corresponding *malaise* — an agonized and self-conscious restlessness. Mr. J. Isaacs in his *Assessment of Twentieth Century Literature* wrote: 'Kierkegaard is the grandfather of modern anxiety, as Kafka is its father', and this is certainly true of Kierkegaard. Another critic, Miss Dorothy Bassett, has said of him that his 'legacy to twentieth century writers has been a revulsion from mass man; a sense of guilt and the necessity for atonement; realization of loss and longing for a new expression for spiritual verities; and the growing conviction that man, instead of being perfectible and master of his fate, *is the victim of uncontrollable forces.*'

The concluding words, which I have italicized, need to be

examined. They are a just interpretation of a great part of modern writing and are, I believe, the reason why that writing, even when most brilliant, has the appearance of frenzy and disease.

To say, as the Greeks did, that man is in the hands of Fate, was to see man religiously, as part of a great though mysterious design. To see man, as Thomas Hardy often did, as a creature who was the 'sport' of 'the President of the Immortals', was still to see him religiously — Hardy, for all his agnosticism, being an inescapably religious man. To see man, as the Prayer Book does, as 'the child of God' is certainly to acknowledge that he is not ultimately and independently 'master of his fate', although, under God, he exercises free-will. But all these points of view are fundamentally different from the point of view of a writer who considers man as a *victim of uncontrollable forces*.

The word *victim* implies self-pity; the word *uncontrollable* implies an impious and arrogant desire to control the forces that created us. This arrogance and this self-pity lie at the root of what I have called the 'agonized and self-conscious restlessness' of a great part of modern literature — and of modern life. We have bred a generation of self-pitying Satans, of petty disciples of Prometheus, who do not even believe in the gods against whom they rebel. And this is true, by a bitter paradox, not only of the materialists who follow Sartre and not Kierkegaard, but even of certain writers who, though they adhere to the Christian faith, only too evidently are incapable of the Christian acceptances and write in tormented exile from the peace of God.

So our civilization is tearing itself and disintegrating itself.

.    .    .    .

If I say that this is unnecessary, I shall be accused of being smoothly complacent. Nevertheless it is true that, unless all history and all wisdom and all faith are lies, the opportunities of good are perpetual. They have not suddenly been withdrawn from our age. Because we call ourselves 'modern man' we have not ceased to be man. We are no more 'victims' than our forefathers, and grace is as accessible to us as it was to them.

The greatest need of our age is to make itself accessible to grace by releasing itself from the pressure of its fears, its anxieties, its self-pity, and allowing itself to be renewed. There are a thousand ways of doing this but none can be prescribed; each man has to find or, rather, has to recognize his own when it is opened before him. The essential condition is a release of the mind from its habitual, modernistic obsessions.

It is not necessary to be in the intellectual fashion. It is not necessary to admire, or even to read, the book that is being widely discussed. It is not necessary to join a league for the advocacy of This or the suppression of That. It is not necessary to think in terms of Contemporary Values. The phrase is a convenient one in conversation, but there are no Contemporary Values; there are only Values; just as there are no Modern Women and no Modern Art, but only women and art. Art is not a competition between periods or between groups. Dickens is not a bad writer because Jane Austen is a good one, or Poe a bad poet because T. S. Eliot has different merits. Art is always news of reality that cannot be expressed in other terms. It is timeless, as man is timeless. Only the distorting glass of our contemporary obsession makes us see them otherwise.

To remove that distorting glass from before our eyes is

not to 'escape' from life, but to see it anew. In that fresh vision, we ourselves are re-created. By this means, and by this means only, can our civilization be renewed. It was precisely by this means — by man's refusal to be embedded in ideas then fashionable and contemporary, by his ability to take Time Out from Today and to re-value human life in terms of the spirit — that the great revolutions of the mind have been accomplished. The Renaissance was Time Out from mediaevalism and a rebirth of the wisdom of ancient Greece. Progress is never a mechanical step forward from today; it is a recapitulation of experience, an act of imagination and judgement.

# A DEFENCE OF STORY-TELLING *

OF late years, the world's production of stories has pro-
digiously increased. They are told on screen and on stage,
in books and magazines and newspapers. They are advertised as nothing but soap was advertised in my boyhood,
and there seems to be scarcely a woman in England or
America that has not a manuscript under her arm. Against
production of this kind there was bound to be a revolt of
opinion.

I would not if I could suppress this revolt. To consider in
what way, with what motive and equipment many of these
stories are written is to wish that the writers of them would
earn a more honest living in a less speculative trade. It happens to be true that great stories have been composed by
people whom a scholastic board would describe as 'unqualified'; it is therefore rashly assumed that no apprenticeship
is necessary and that anyone is entitled to write a book who
has an inkpot and a grievance. It was bad enough when the
fashion in authorship was for novels and plays. Most of the
plays did not see the light for the comfortable reason that
the production of plays is expensive, and we were in some
degree protected even from the novels by the simple fact
that the worst of plots requires a little patience to give it
continuity. The immediate future is more alarming.

* A lecture delivered at the Royal Institution of Great Britain,
February 1934.

Autobiography is being treated as a branch of novel writing. A cloud of confession hangs over us which will presently burst in a storm of erotic self-pity. Every woman is at heart a Rousseau, and nothing could be more lamentable than to have Rousseau's impulses without his genius. It was once considered desirable to learn how to live and how to write before attempting an autobiography. Now every schoolgirl knows that she carries her confessions in her pillowcase, and that, unlike Lord Byron, she has only to go to bed one night to find herself famous.

For this reason, among others, imaginative authorship has fallen into disrepute. It is not, heaven knows, neglected. It is flattered and advertised as it has never been. Doubtless there are authors who, whether they personally delight in it or not, accept this drum-beating as evidence that the importance of their art is being recognized by the modern world. In truth, it is evidence of nothing but the world's unfailing reaction to all forms of notoriety. The drum is beaten, not in honour of the work of art, but in clamour for the man whose name and photograph have become hypnotically familiar. People stare at him as they stare at the walls of a house in which a murder has been committed. They invite him to dinner as they would invite a murderer to dinner if they could. This is nothing new. There has never been a time when the vulgar would not run out from a tragedy to witness a hanging. We have to accept this and make the best of it; it would be a waste of time to attempt a defence of story-telling against such attentions as these. But it is worth while to defend it against the coldness, I would say almost the suspicious contempt, with which it is often treated by discriminating men and women whose collective opinion is, in fact, the opinion of their age.

An artist who makes, in a world which is, or pretends that it is, predominantly interested in science, the highest possible claim for his own art is treading upon very dangerous ground. Nevertheless I claim that story-telling is among the supreme activities of the human mind, co-equal with those activities to which the greatest men of science have devoted their lives; that by it truth is made known; and that, altogether apart from any direct influence it may have upon conduct, it is as necessary and, in the most exalted sense, as useful, as any service to mankind in which the genius of the race has been engaged.

How formidable and how consistent the distrust of story-telling has been is made clear in all the pages of history. The Greeks alone seem to have been relatively exempt from it, and even among the Greeks Plato would not accord to poets a place in his Republic. When classical learning, in the last days of the Roman Empire and after the Empire's disruption, was fighting a losing battle with Christian innovation, the distrust, the fear of story-telling in all its many forms became insistent. It did not cease to be beloved; it has never ceased to be beloved; but the leaders of contemporary thought, even while they loved it and secretly devoured it, spoke of it continually with misgiving, as of a temptation that good men should resist.

Miss Helen Waddell, in her book on *The Wandering Scholars*, quotes many instances of this prejudice, and among them that of Jerome. 'The songs of the poets are the food of demons,' he says, '. . . their suavity is a delight to all men. . . . The very priests of God are reading comedies, singing the love songs of the Bucolics, turning over Virgil; and that which was a necessity in boyhood, they make the guilty pleasure of their maturity.' Nearly a thousand years later, in 1285, Nicholas, Chancellor of the University of Paris, said: 'We are in danger, we who read the writings of the pagan poets.' The danger perceived in pagan literature was not only, and not chiefly, that it was heretical, but that it was so often beautiful and, as the grave churchmen thought, a diversion from the quest of God. 'By some, I know not what, factious bond,' exclaimed the preacher of a university sermon in Toulouse in 1229, 'lust and literature cling together,' and we have been told how the abbess of Hohenberg 'made an ingenious sketch for her nuns, a rose window design of Philosophy with Plato and Socrates at her feet, the seven liberal arts in a circle, but in the corners of the page are four figures inscribing naughtiness, the poets, the magicians, the idle story-tellers, each inspired by a lean black fowl of portentous neck, who sits on his shoulder and whispers in his ear.'

It is unnecessary to pursue this attitude of mind through the centuries. Sometimes it is the Catholic Church that warns mankind against story-tellers; sometimes it is Puritanism that banishes stage plays from the sight of the godly; sometimes it is commerce enthroned that contemptuously leaves novel-reading to its womenfolk who treat it, and are expected to treat it, as they treat gossip, a box of chocolates or a hand at cards. Lady Blessington, who admired Bulwer and read him with delight, was inclined to pity him because the novel was a medium beneath what she considered to be the true level of his powers. 'Authors like Mr. Bulwer,' she said, 'whose minds are overflowing with genius, are compelled to make fiction the vehicle for giving to the public thoughts and opinions that are deserving of a higher grade of literature.' Even the ages that have done conspicuous honour to their story-tellers have done it in the spirit of one who raises the pay of his housemaid. With the possible exception of Voltaire, Dickens was more honoured in his lifetime than any writer, but whose occupation was considered to be the more serious, his or Gladstone's? Not long ago a play was performed that had for its subject the life of Carlyle. When he spoke of the agony and labour that the first volume of his *French Revolution* had cost him, the audience received his remark with respectful sympathy. He was a historian, and historians are to be taken seriously, like politicians, lawyers and men of science. But when a novelist, who happened to be present on the stage, said that she also had suffered in the composition of her tale, the audience laughed heartily. Why? Partly, it is true, because she was Geraldine Jewsbury, a slightly ridiculous person, but chiefly, I am sure, because a modern audience does not differ from its predecessors in regarding novel-writing as a very trivial occupation.

The acknowledged leaders of thought today, corresponding to the churchmen and puritans of the past, are beyond question the men of science, the economists, the biologists, the sociologists and the political theorists. These are the modern hierarchy, and all over the world the most intelligent and vital members of the younger generation sit at their feet. What is their attitude to the art of story-telling? It is very clearly indicated in the extraordinary cult of the detective story among them. Though Oxford, like the Greeks, is comparatively exempt, there is said to be scarcely a science don at Cambridge or a bluestocking in Bloomsbury who does not prop a detective-novel against the coffee-pot. Their reason is not that they love the art of fiction, but that they despise it. A detective-novel is a thing apart. It is not, and does not pretend to be, a work of art; it is an exercise in ingenuity, and the reading of it is comparable with the solving of a crossword puzzle. The dons read it, not because they are bloodthirsty, but because, if blood appears in it at all, it appears on the carpet as a clue and not in the veins of the characters as a stimulus to imagination. There is, certainly, no harm in reading books of this kind. I happen to find them unreadable, but that is no reason for condemning them, for I have the same impatience of bridge, of crossword puzzles and indeed of all semi-intellectual means of wasting time. But every man is entitled to his own method of relaxation, and I take it to be no worse to read a detective story than to play trains on the nursery floor. The interest of the practice lies in its special implications. If I play trains on the nursery floor, I do not boast about it, but among learned men the reading of detective stories is a foible of which they are inordinately proud. They discuss the stories with other learned men; they compare the points of one story with the points of another; they make a paraded affectation of the whole affair. Ask them of a book by Huxley or Thomas Mann and they say: 'I am afraid I read no fiction but detective stories,' and they await a snigger of applause. Why? Because they wish it to be understood that, though they are willing to read nonsense in odd moments, they are not such fools as to take imaginative literature seriously.

This is one angle of contempt. Another is even more remarkable. There are many people, particularly very young people, belonging generally to the political Left, who are careful to distinguish between pure story-telling and story-telling with a social content. I do not wish to misrepresent them by suggesting that they will admire no story that is not party propaganda, though this is too often the spirit of their criticism. Their more moderate argument is, roughly, this: that it is one of the principal duties of a novel to reflect, if not the manners, at any rate the spirit of its age; that romantic individualism, because the world is tending more and more to one form or another of the collectivist state, is dead; that the two dominating problems of our day are economic inequality and the prevention of war; and that novels which are not given over to the discussion of these problems are frivolous and indeed anti-social. The catch-word is social-consciousness. Social-consciousness has been dragged in to do service as an aesthetic value. Truth and Beauty are considered to be old-fashioned tests in the estimate of a work of art, which must, to be regarded seriously, have a social-revolutionary core.

This point of view may be easily understood. Pure story-telling — a love story, for example, such as *Tristan and Iseult* or *Manon Lescaut* or Turgenev's *First Love* — is regarded as a drug. It gives pleasure and, therefore, like vodka in Russia, tends to blunt the edge of a desirable discontent. It leads men to look inwards upon their own souls, or, looking outward, to discover at once the beauty of individual experience and the vanity of collective endeavour. To read the great stories of the world is to realize more and more that the world is improved, and can be improved, very little by collective and deliberate action. It affects the fringe of manners; it exchanges one man's poverty for another man's riches; it checks the tyranny of kings to establish the tyranny of dictators; it puts more money into men's pockets and then depreciates its value in terms of goods; it increases the speed of transport and proportionately increases the distances that a man must travel each day to his business. Meanwhile man's happiness or unhappiness, his value or worthlessness, depends upon his private philosophy — on his power to love and to respond to love, on his faculty of pleasure in little things, on his belief or disbelief in heaven and hell, on his capacity for hope and acceptance — in brief on the nature and strength of his secret imagination. Story-telling and poetry teach him this and teach it continually. They make of economic theory not a burning faith but, philosophically, a matter of indifference. They lead men to say that they would rather have written Gray's *Elegy* than take Quebec; they lead men to think that, since eternity is long and youth short, they would rather win their lady than the Bastille. Prisons, say the great story-tellers, are always rebuilt; ladies, unfortunately, are not. Prisons, say the story-tellers again, are not set up by a man's environment but by himself, by his fears, his hatreds, his jealousies, his weaknesses, and there is no escape from them except in his own contemplative wisdom or in the three great acts of transcendence — love, poetry and death. Very naturally those who wish to use mankind as the material of collective experiment, dislike all stories that do not awaken a belligerent social-consciousness. For precisely the same reason the Walrus and the Carpenter would have condemned romantic individualism among oysters.

The objections to story-telling, then, may be summarized as follows. First, there is the feeling of plain men that a story is a luxury and an entertainment, a means of wasting time more or less pleasantly. Second, there is the general objection of men of science and the leaders of contemporary thought that story-telling is inexact, that indulgence in it produces irrelevant and confusing emotions, that it does not advance the truth and that it must not, therefore, be taken seriously. Third, there is the objection of those who, while admitting that certain stories have been, and may still be, powerful instruments of reform, sincerely believe that, in the present condition of the world, a purely aesthetic novel is anti-social because it does nothing to advance, and may even retard, improvement of human conditions. It is a very formidable indictment.

To answer it by an examination of the great novels of the past and their influence on human destiny would be to fall into confusion and to invite the retort that they are, after all, of the past, and that it is with the present that we are concerned. To brandish great names and to ask whether Shakespeare or Newton did the greater service to God and man would be to indulge in vain rhetoric. There is no way to attack the infinite complexity of this moral and aesthetic problem except at its philosophic root.

Men have always been profoundly concerned to speculate on the nature of reality, and not philosophers only. The plainest and, in his own view, the most materialistic of men, who would mock at any suggestion that he was a metaphysician, nevertheless speculates on reality by implication whenever he proudly denies his belief in anything but what his senses directly communicate to him; and at the opposite extreme, the most devout of men who, having deliberately put enquiry away from him, accepts without question the dogma of some sect, is, without fully realising it, speculating by proxy, for all dogmas spring from and have their differences in opposed views of what is real and what is unreal. Faith and conduct have their origin here. If a man believes that only the bodies of things are real, he will behave and think in one way; if he believes that minds as well as bodies are real, he will behave in another; if he believes that with minds and bodies the total reality is not complete, but that there is a third component, which we may call the supernatural, he will behave in another. He will behave differently in each instance because in each instance he will think differently. By his theory of reality his whole system of values will be affected.

What is real and what unreal I do not propose to argue here. The point upon which I wish to insist is that the process by which a man arrives at his theory of reality is not, and cannot be, a strict argument from cause to effect or from effect to cause. He cannot in this, as in other matters, build securely on a basis of observed fact, because the reality of his observation is one of the questions he has to decide. For this reason there cannot be a strictly scientific proof of any theory of reality. A man who insists upon such a proof must admit that he is without a theory, and yet, if he have no theory of what is real, his values are without root and his conduct is empirical merely.

If reasoned conduct depends upon values, and reasoned values depend upon a persuasion of what is real, and a persuasion of what is real can be arrived at only with the aid of imagination and not by scientific argument alone, does it not inevitably follow that the whole of a man's being, from his least outward act to his innermost contact with his God, has its key to an imaginative process?

In what way does the imagination operate? For the greater part of most men's lives, it operates over a fairly wide range but on a single plane. As memory, it recalls the past to him; as fear or greed or hope it anticipates the future, working always on or very near the surface of his experience. Even its researches below the surface, of which the psycho-therapists speak, though they penetrate the crust of his conscious mind, do not, in the eye of eternity, go very far; and it will be observed that though from a man at a given instant of his life the shafts of imagination move forward into the future or backward into the past, they do not ordinarily strike into the present. He is lifting a glass of wine to his lips; he imagines what its taste will be; he imagines what the taste of a similar wine has been in the past; the wine reaches his tongue and again his imagination flies out forward and back — in recollection of other pleasures associated with this pleasure or of penalties that he has paid for it and may have to pay again. In the immediate present, he is given over to the operation of his sense of taste and does not imagine at all. Because he *is* tasting the wine, he ceases to imagine it.

But, it will be said, what is there for him to imagine? The taste, the actuality, has displaced the former image of it. The answer is that, in the poised instant, he may by imagination be carried beyond the idea of this particular wine to the idea of wine as such. I have chosen a commonplace example of what I believe to be an important truth — that imagination is the means, and the only means, by which man may proceed from sensuous knowledge of the particular to intuitive apprehension of the universal. This is the key to imaginative writing. This is what is called — I think misleadingly — the creative act of an artist. An artist is one who has developed in high degree this imaginative faculty of penetrating the appearances of things and of discovering their vital essence. Nor, except in its intensity, is this process exceptional. Everyone is aware of it at special and memorable instants of his life. Outside your house there is a path through a wood with, at its end, an open prospect of sky and valley. Ordinarily, as you walk down this path on a summer's day, your feeling is of gladness that the leaves are green and, at the end, that the view is beautiful. One day

G

your mood changes. You feel that the world is brilliant and shining; your gladness becomes joy, your joy almost exaltation; you feel, not physical well-being only, but spiritual well-being; the present rushes in upon you and becomes intensified; you have a sense of penetration beyond the appearances of things; through your pleasure in the green wood wells up, like water from the earth, a pleasure in greenness itself, and through your customary delight in the loveliness of the countryside comes an apprehension of beauty itself. These moments of heightened perception come to the simplest of men. They do not express it, perhaps, in the terms in which I have expressed it. They do not say that they have perceived greenness itself or beauty itself; probably they say nothing at all; but they know that their life has been enriched, and, if they remember the instant, they are made by it more sensitive to similar impressions in themselves and more charitable to them in others. These experiences, though most men are too modest to claim them as such, are of the same kind with the experiences of saints and artists, though not of the same degree of intensity.

They take many forms. One of these forms is the experience of mathematicians, whose apprehension sometimes mysteriously outruns their logical processes. All of us who, in the humblest way, have trod the foothills of higher mathematics, know what it is now and then to become aware of the solution of a problem without having gone through the steps by which ordinarily that solution would have been approached, and I suggest very tentatively that men who are to me, in the world of mathematics, what I am in the world of literature to a child learning to spell, have almost certainly had experience of direct mathematical apprehension which has caused them to feel, if but for a moment, that they were in contact with truths outside the present range of their intellects.

But the mathematical form of this experience is beyond the reach of most of us. There are other and more familiar forms of it. Perhaps the commonest is that which I have described — an experience related to flowers and wood and sky and earth. Even a motorist is capable of such an experience who, while going at eighty miles an hour, enters into the idea of speed. Certainly, when we are young, we are mysteriously capable of it — first in our childhood and again when we fall in love.

It is the general habit of the world to laugh at lovers, to say that they are mad, to treat them as if they were beings temporarily removed from the plane of ordinary life; and in this the world is more right than it knows. If love were no more than an excitement of the senses pursuing a biological sequence from cause to effect, what would there be to laugh at? Where then would madness appear? If love were this alone, it would be no more amusing or mysterious or mad than hunger, and would not appear to be so. The truth is that young lovers *are* removed from the plane of ordinary life. Common things shine for them. They feel that the earth was created only as a scene for their love and is, in that sense, unreal. The cant phrases about lovers are, for them, true — that they 'see each other with new eyes' or that 'the world is made new for them'. From our point of view they are bewitched, they are 'translated' like poor Bottom in *A Midsummer Night's Dream*; from their point of view we are stricken with blindness. What has happened? Their imagination has ceased to be sluggish as ours commonly is. It is quick, fiery, powerful, penetrative of the instant. It has revealed to them, in whatever beauty each may possess, the radiance of another and universal beauty. They are — to use the word in the strict meaning of its Greek derivation — in an ecstasy: 'out of their senses'. Two of the most familiar lines of Shelley precisely express this idea of the universals that lie, or are felt to lie, behind particular experiences:

> Life, like a dome of many-coloured glass,
> Stains the white radiance of eternity.

Sometimes the dome ceases to be opaque. The radiance shines through. Imagination, when brilliant and vital, clears the glass; imagination that is dull and sluggish clouds it. All this, I submit, is not a matter of exceptional experience known only to mystical saints and great artists. It is, though rarely perhaps and in mild degree, the common experience of mankind.

But the tendency of the human imagination is to congeal. A thousand influences produce this tendency, particularly in a modern world. Independence of character, a bold individualism in thought and behaviour, is becoming increasingly rare. Uniformity of education, standardised environment, that doubtful blessing — speed of communication, films, wireless, above all the extreme difficulty of solitude — these things, which, from one point of view, are progressive, make more and more for the standardization of man and the attachment of spurious prides to material things. To put it briefly, he is desperately afraid of being a freak. He dresses, speaks and thinks as others dress, speak and think. He is afraid to imagine. He shuts himself up in a little prison of conventional negations. His thought springs from catchword to catchword as the popular newspapers may dictate. At one moment his catchword is science — and science means for him faster and faster movement. He does not ask why or whither. When his newspaper tells him that another 'record' has been broken, he goes through, like an automaton, all the emotions of rejoicing. At another moment, his catchword is psycho-analysis, which enables him to say, whenever any discussion arises about the character of his neighbour or the nature of his God, 'probably it has a sexual origin', whereupon, having at best proceeded one thousandth part of the way towards the first cause, he ceases to exercise his imagination further. All that he has done, in his worship of catchwords, is to give to mediaeval fetishes twentieth-century names, and to set up new barriers against imaginative meditation. It is one of the functions of story-telling to break these barriers down, to unfreeze the imaginative stream, to enable it to flow again.

The way in which a great story or any genuine work of art operates to this end is by an awakening of the aesthetic passion. What precisely the aesthetic passion is has been made excellently clear by a writer to whom every artist owes a great debt, Professor Alexander, in his *Beauty and other Forms of Value*. It is to be carefully distinguished from the emotions provoked by the subject of a work of art. It is the emotion that springs from apprehension of beauty as such, or, to return to my previous line of thought, it is the perception of a universal within and behind the particular. What excites the spectator of a Greek statue of Aphrodite is not an emotion connected with its subject — not its precise resemblance to a woman, for neither in colour nor in shape does it resemble her as closely as many a trumpery piece of figure-painting exhibited in Bond Street; nor any erotic stimulus occasioned by it, for nothing is less erotic or more austere than a Greek masterpiece; nor any power of sentimental or religious association, for Aphrodite is not a

goddess of ours. What excites him is not even an apprehension of the artist's technical mastery of his medium, for
most men are ignorant of the difficulties, and are therefore
dead to the triumphs, of carving. What excites him is,
simply, that the statue is a means of communication between
him and the universals. So it is in other arts. They make
man aware of the universals; they permit his imagination to
flow; they uncurtain the window of that narrow room which
is his mortal life.

This, it may be said, is a very dangerous process, unless
there is a guarantee that his imagination will flow in the
right direction. Is there any such guarantee? Certainly there
is none that his imagination will flow in a direction that con-
forms with any given theory of conduct, and, from their
own point of view, those conservative parents are fully
justified who say that novels 'put ideas into young people's
heads'. A story is not a moral agent, it is not an educational
agent, and people who praise the drama as educational are
praising it for its accidents, not for its essence; nor is art, as
the later Tolstoy argued, an agent of utility. A great story is
an imaginative flux — that is all. And that, in my view, is
everything.

To examine the means by which a story acts as a flux
would be to embark upon another and harder essay than
this. I have already treated of this subject, in its relation to
the theatre, in an essay on *The Nature of Dramatic Illusion*,
and will content myself here with saying what may serve as
an indication of a line of thought rather than as a formal
pursuit of it.

There is a distinction between doing the work of imagination *for* a reader and enabling his own imagination to flow.
If I write in such a way that a reader feels that he is in the

room I describe and that he hears the words I have set down on paper, I have done no more than create a perfect delusion — a difficult exercise in artistic naturalism, but one which does not entitle the performer of it to claim more than that he is a competent craftsman. But if, with or without perfect delusion, I can, by the love story I tell, liberate the reader's own imagination in such a way that he has, after reading my story, a livelier insight into love itself than he had before, if I can for a moment cause his own spirit to move across my page and inhabit a plane of reality of which formerly he has had but momentary and doubtful glimpses, then I am a great artist. I am, of course, so far as a particular reader is concerned, working in the dark. I do not know who he is: I do not know the nature of his imagination; I could not if I would, work to produce a specified influence upon him, and I would not if I could. All that a story-teller can do is to see his own story as a glass through which the light of the universals appears to him, and to keep that glass clear. To keep it faultlessly clear is to write a masterpiece that endures from generation to generation; to allow it to be thick and continue to write is to produce hack-work.

There is a very happy instance of what I mean in *The Metamorphoses* of Apuleius, one of the earliest surviving examples of prose fiction, often called *The Golden Ass*. This book is for the most part an account of the adventures of one Lucius, the narrator, who was by magic turned into an ass. He served many masters, and the chapters of his life have little connexion except in his identity; they are, moreover, supplemented by anecdotes, short and long, which have nothing to do with the main story and having probably done duty before the days of Apuleius, have served since as the basis of certain tales of Boccaccio. In the Elizabethan translation, the whole of Apuleius is exceedingly good to read, in much the same way that Fielding is good to read; but neither Apuleius nor Fielding wrote an aesthetic novel. They told delicious tales, they had a glorious power of invention, and they were, by remote implication, moralists, and these things in themselves seem to me a justification of having lived; but if anyone is disposed to attack Apuleius or Fielding — or Jane Austen for that matter — on the ground that they were what the abbess of Hohenberg depicted as 'idle story-tellers', I am not disposed to defend them. They do not, that is to say, find shelter within my special fortress. They have defences of their own; it would be arrogant and foolish to deny the title of 'artist' to them; but they are not, except on rare occasions, artists in the sense that they have power to communicate the universals. To this there is, in Apuleius, a sudden and brilliant exception. He breaks off from his main narrative to tell the story of Cupid and Psyche, and, while this interlude continues, the reader is translated to an imaginative plane altogether different from that on which he has been following the ass's adventures among robbers and courtesans. Hitherto, in reading, one has danced along on the plane of entertainment; suddenly at the names of Cupid and Psyche, an enchantment falls upon the tale and the reader's own imagination takes wing.

This, then, is the case for story-telling — not that it entertains or informs or educates, though it may do all this, but that it revitalizes the reader's perception of reality, it fluidifies his imagination of the universals, making him aware by intuition of the nature of things. Here the connexion appears between story-telling and scientific research, between story-telling and religious aspiration. All three are ultimately concerned to discover the nature of things, and, in

the discovery, to lead man, the discoverer, towards equili-
brium and fullness of life. In *The Foundations of Aesthetics*,
written in 1922 by Ogden Richards and James Wood, these
words occur: 'As we realize beauty we become more fully
ourselves the more our impulses are engaged. . . . Through
no other experience can the full richness and complexity of
our environment be realized. The ultimate value of equili-
brium is that it is better to be fully than partially alive.'
Gentile, in *The Philosophy of Art*, approaching the same
problem from a different angle, for he will admit no reality
external to the process of thought, nevertheless reaches this
conclusion:

'In a work of art the feeling is everything. For the feeling is
the form in which the subject matter is fused and transfigured.
. . . The critic who still distinguishes a subject-matter, with a
value of its own, from the form with which it is identified, and
from which alone it gets form and actuality, is still upon the
threshold of art and has not the key to unlock the door. The
truth is that, if the hymnslive, the gods live too; they live in the
hymns.'

And the late Poet Laureate said this:

Beauty is the highest of all these occult influences,
the quality of appearances that thru' the sense
wakeneth spiritual emotion in the mind of man:
And Art, as it createth new forms of beauty,
awakeneth new ideas that advance the spirit
in the life of Reason to the wisdom of God.

The saying, 'Art, as it *createth* new forms of beauty,
awakeneth new ideas' is, I think, open to misinterpretation.
Beauty I conceive to be absolute and universal, an aspect of
God. Art does not create beauty; it reveals beauty, the universal, by making statues, stories, pictures which have the
effect of lifting the darkness, as it were a curtain, from the
glass through which man sees. What Shelley said of poetry

is applicable to aesthetic story-telling. 'Poetry,' he said. 'lifts the veil from the hidden beauty of the world,' and he proceeded to argue — and his own poetry at its best and worst was rich in proofs of his argument — that 'the effect of poetry is diminished in exact proportion to the strength of its moral aim'. So in story-telling. It must stand or fall as an instrument of pure imagination, as one of the means by which man is enabled, as Shelley says, 'to imagine intensely and comprehensively', as precisely that which Jerome thought it was not — a revelation of God because it is a revelation of the nature of man. If we seek to defend it on the grounds of worldly utility, we shall be overwhelmed as Tolstoy has been overwhelmed, but if we believe that there is value in love, in poetry, in mystical apprehension, then our position is unassailable, for the value of story-telling is the same with theirs. It is a raising of curtains, an opening of windows, an admittance of light.

# DIALOGUE IN NOVELS AND PLAYS*

*Many senior members of P.E.N. are better qualified than I am to speak of Hermon Ould's services as its secretary. For my part, I find it pleasant to recall that he was not only an organizer but an originating artist with a special interest in the theatre. In my early days he was highly thought of as an experimentalist, a good deal influenced, and I think handicapped, by the German Expressionist techniques. He had not what may perhaps be called 'the gift of large audiences' — a phrase which I use neither in praise nor in blame; but the absence of that gift is discouraging, and it is a mark of Hermon Ould's quality that he never allowed it either to embitter him or to dull his interest in the theatre itself. Last time we met — when we ought to have been earnestly discussing the affairs of some Committee — what the Committee was about I have forgotten, but it was certainly a tedious and frustrate Committee, for all committees are except those over which Miss Wedgwood graciously presides — Hermon Ould and I, before the Minutes had been read and after the Committee had dutifully decided to decide nothing at all, took to the theatre as ducks to water. We began with Strindberg and went on to a discussion of dialogue in general, and I remember how his face lighted up and with how much knowledge and eagerness he talked. It was a subject near to his private, as distinct from his secretarial, heart. That is why I have chosen it. What I have to say, in this memorial lecture, is in a sense a development of my conversation with him.*

As soon as I had chosen this subject, I began to see how fortunate and how rash I had been: fortunate because it interested me more and more and led me on farther and farther into the theory of novels and plays; and rash because a subject so far-reaching and so exploratory is not easy to discuss without either too much complexity or too much simplification. Indeed I feel a little as Lady Bracknell might

* The Hermon Ould Memorial Lecture, 1953, delivered under the auspices of the English Centre of the P.E.N. Club.

have done, in *The Importance of Being Earnest,* if she had been required to lecture to Miss Cecily Cardew on the facts of life. Dialogue is an analogous subject. It has a deceptive appearance of superficiality. Anyone can chatter, just as anyone can flirt. But the moment one begins to distinguish between good chatter and bad chatter or between virtuous and unvirtuous flirtation, one is plunged into a study of convention, of morals, of contemporary manners, above all of style. But on the whole I am glad that, of the two subjects, mine is dialogue. In flirtation, style is of outrageous importance, and nothing could be more difficult to illustrate on a lecture-platform.

We are all aware that three of the principal uses of dialogue are the advancement of narrative, the demonstration of character and the creation of atmosphere or mood. Any one of these subjects would provide material for a library of criticism, but they are too wide and large to fit conveniently into a single lecture. We may, however, observe this — and it is an important distinction to make — that whereas a novelist is free to eliminate dialogue altogether or, if he pleases, to use it only now and then to 'point' his story-telling, a dramatist is completely reliant upon it. A novel moreover is five or six times the length of a play and may be much longer. It follows that one of the highest merits of dramatic dialogue, particularly when there is a complex story to tell, is its power to pull several strings at the same time — the strings of narrative, of character, of mood. It must also pull the strings of the past and of the present *at the same time.* A novelist may legitimately suspend his present action and indulge in retrospect, but a dramatist, once launched, cannot do this because he has no means of suspending his present action or at any rate his audience's demand for it. If, then, retrospect is necessary to him, he has to use methods of extreme delicacy and guile — methods, if I may say so, much more delicate and adroit than those used by Pinero in the first act of *The Second Mrs. Tanqueray* where retrospect creaks. He must so design his dialogue that each line, while advancing the present action, little by little and almost imperceptibly admits us to knowledge of the past. The classic example is Ibsen's *Rosmersholm*.

The task is of extreme difficulty and is made almost impossible if the theatre is large and the audience — I will not say stupid and lazy, but disinclined to intellectual effort. Ibsen gives all the right hints — but they are *hints*; if we are handing round tea-trays we are lost. The retrospective knowledge he offers us is *offered*, not — in the brutal language of the theatre — 'planted' again and again. In brief, great dialogue assumes a certain responsive intelligence in its audience. For example, if our heroine, while arranging flowers, happens to say casually that she dislikes the smell of lilies because they remind her of Aunt Matilda's funeral, that should be enough; it ought not to be necessary to tell the tea-trays again and again that Aunt Matilda is dead. And yet, in a sense, it is necessary if Aunt Matilda's death is of great importance. A dramatist, unless he is an incompetent amateur, will always conform to the conditions of the theatre. If either in retrospect or present action he has something to say that is unusual or peculiarly subtle he will take care to say it, in different forms, more than once, for even the most intelligent playgoer may miss a point now and then. And in the theatre we cannot turn back, as we turn back the pages of a book.

For corresponding reasons, a wise novelist will often avoid the use of dialogue on occasions where a dramatist has to use it because he has no alternative. Here I venture to give an example from my own experience. In a play of mine, *The Flashing Stream*, a naval officer had to explain to a girl the idea of an invention — an aerial homing torpedo dirigible by wireless and by sound vibration. This idea is now familiar to you all, for my prophecy has been unfortunately fulfilled; but in 1938 it was completely unfamiliar both to the girl on the stage and to the whole audience. I had somehow to 'get it across'. In a novel, the nature of the invention could have been made clear by the narrative method, dialogue being used, if at all, only for lightening or pointing the explanation. On the stage, the only available means was dialogue, and the difficulties of brevity, lightness and lucidity were extreme. I speak of it only to make this point: there are many scenes where people are talking together, in which the novelist's freedom to get away from direct speech is a godsend to him. He can either slide gracefully away into indirect speech which gives him a chance to compress and summarize; or he can, at will, suspend the dialogue and use plain narrative. A dramatist can do none of this; he has to go on in dialogue. You and I know quite well that when my naval officer was explaining his invention to the girl, their conversation would have been long and very often repetitive. She would have asked questions; he would have gone over the ground again; gradually they would have fogged the thing out between them. The stage dialogue had to preserve the illusion of their natural conversation and yet to differ from it in almost every respect — in speed, in directness, in continuity and economy. And that brings me to the aspect of dialogue that I want chiefly to consider this evening — I mean, dialogue in its relationship to conversation.

·　　·　　·　　·

It is impossible to think of dialogue without thinking also of conversation, and I will say at once that I shall use the word 'conversation' for the talk of men and women in ordinary life, and the word 'dialogue' for the talk of characters in novels and plays. Though the connexion between the two is much more remote and complex than is generally supposed, a connexion exists and we must examine it.

Conversation can be charming as an entertainment, but as a means of self-expression, still more as a means of intercommunication, it is extremely inadequate. Man is a creature who lives alone from birth to death. Even from those with whom he is most intimate he remains divided by impassable barriers; ego and ego do not combine. He lives as it were in a house on wheels which moves with him from place to place, from experience to experience, but which remains — according to his range — the palace or the prison of his individuality. Now and then in the supreme moments of his life — in his poetry, in his love, and, I think, in his death — the walls of his house dissolve or seem to dissolve; but of those supreme moments I need say only, in this context, that, whatever else they are, they are not conversational. And when the supreme moments of poetry and love are over, he finds himself again in his little house and begins to chatter again, just as Coleridge, after his voyage in a painted ship upon a painted ocean and his taste of the milk of Paradise, sat down to years and years of table-talk, signifying a great deal (for Coleridge's little house was never less than a house of genius) and yet, by comparison with his moments of illumination, signifying nothing. And so Coleridge, like the rest of us, tried from within his house to communicate. He looked out of the window, using the faculty of sight; he stretched out his hand, using the faculty of touch; and he employed, as best he could, his marvellous gift of talk. And yet, how inadequate that gift was, even in him! How much more inadequate in the rest of us! Language, even the whole language in the use of a great master, is no match for the infinite complexities of thought and feeling. Conversation, in which you and I improvise upon a vocabulary of a few hundred words, is only a clumsy use of a clumsy code. As a means of communication, it differs in degree but scarcely in kind from the barking of dogs or the yowling of cats, and they are assisted by a sense of smell which in us is sadly deteriorated. Indeed, I am inclined to think that cats have conversational advantages over us. They are not inhibited by our tendency to understatement. They do not confine themselves, on amorous occasions, to a casual cliché and an inarticulate gasp. They do not, like the most approved modern actors, throw away their lines. Many a time and oft, in such a night as this, I have heard them, in my London garden, run the whole gamut of comedy and tragedy from Venice to Verona, from Illyria to Glamis. I scarcely know whether I am listening to conversation or to dialogue, to improvisation or to art. One of the more glorious secrets of feline life is, I think, that cats rehearse their love-scenes — a practice which may be recommended to young men and women nowadays who, as if they were members of a weekly repertory company, so often undertake, without adequate preparation, the hazards of performance.

However that may be, cats are a lesson to all of us who are students of dialogue. It appears that there are not two cats in the whole world who cannot compose and play a Balcony Scene. Are there two of us who can? Their most eloquent and impassioned dialogue appears to arise naturally from their conversation, as ours certainly does not; and such natural artists are they that, if for any reason the Balcony Scene doesn't go as it should one evening, they change their tempo, their convention, their style, until the lady looking down from the top of the wall is not Juliet but Lady Macbeth.

.     .     .     .

I hope I have now made it clear that it is not the purpose of dialogue to reproduce conversation naturalistically but rather, in the guise of conversation, to supply conversation's deficiencies — to be amusing where conversation is dull, to be economic where conversation is wasteful, to be articulate and lucid where conversation is mumbling or obscure. The method is, of course, the method of all art: intensification by selective discipline and order; and the application of this method by a great master has always, in whatever convention, tragic or frivolous, the same reward — the reward of all art — the discovery, through appearances, of a reality, an essence, underlying them.

At this, you will perhaps rebelliously exclaim: 'It may be all very well to suggest that *Hamlet* leads us to the essence of things, to a reality within appearances, but surely you are not claiming that Congreve's dialogue in *The Way of the World* does anything of the kind?' That is precisely what I do claim. Congreve distils for us the essence of a comic situation. By removing the dross from what would in fact have been the naturalistic talk of Mirabel and Millamant — the hesitations, the superfluities, the blur, the failure of the two speakers to respond to each other and lead each other — Congreve reveals the pure metal of their special perplexity — and the metal sparkles and rings true. The essence of things is not necessarily dark; indeed, I would make bold to say that it never is to the eye of an artist or to the eye of faith.

H

The essence of tragic things certainly is not; for tragedy that is genuinely tragic in vision and in form and not an ugly chaos of violence and self-pity, tragedy that is tragic because it is beautiful and beautiful because it is tragic, is always, always — even the tragedy of *Lear* — a voyage away from the Golden World and, therefore, recalls our minds to its point of departure. And if you are still inclined to believe that, in talking of the reality within appearances, I am talking of some vague philosophical abstraction so gloomy that you would prefer to leave it to the German commentators on *Hamlet*, let me carry you a step further. When Andrew Marvell wrote of

> Annihilating all that's made
> To a green thought in a green shade

he was saying for me what I wish to say. He was penetrating, or annihilating, natural things and arriving at their essence. Dialogue has the same purpose and, at its best, the same reward. And this is true whatever the subject and whatever the convention, tragic, comic or farcical. The essence of gay things is gaiety; of absurd things, absurdity; of light things, lightness of heart. Dialogue is a process of distillation. I shall, perhaps, best illustrate my point with a completely frivolous example: Algernon Moncrieff's second-act entrance in *The Importance of Being Earnest*.

*Enter ALGERNON, very gay and debonair.*

ALGERNON (*raising his hat*). — You are my little cousin Cecily, I'm sure.

CECILY. — You are under some strange mistake. I am not little. In fact, I believe I am more than usually tall for my age. (*Algernon is rather taken aback.*) But I am your cousin Cecily. You, I see from your card, are Uncle Jack's brother, my cousin Ernest, my wicked cousin Ernest.

ALGERNON. — Oh, I am not really wicked at all, cousin Cecily. You mustn't think that I am wicked.

CECILY. — If you are not, then you have certainly been deceiving us all in a very inexcusable manner. I hope you have not been leading a double life, pretending to be wicked and being really good all the time. That would be hypocrisy.

ALGERNON (*looks at her in amazement*). — Oh! Of course I have been rather reckless.

CECILY. — I am glad to hear it.

ALGERNON. — In fact, now you mention the subject, I have been very bad in my own small way.

CECILY. — I don't think you should be so proud of that, though I am sure it must have been very pleasant.

ALGERNON. — It is much pleasanter being here with you.

CECILY. — I can't understand how you are here at all. Uncle Jack won't be back till Monday afternoon.

ALGERNON. — That is a great disappointment. I am obliged to go up by the first train on Monday morning. I have a business appointment that I am anxious . . . to miss!

CECILY. — Couldn't you miss it anywhere but in London?

ALGERNON. — No; the appointment is in London.

CECILY. — Well, I know, of course, how important it is not to keep a business engagement, if one wants to retain any sense of the beauty of life, but still I think you had better wait till Uncle Jack arrives. I know he wants to speak to you about your emigrating.

ALGERNON. — About my what?

CECILY. — Your emigrating. He has gone up to buy your outfit.

ALGERNON. — I certainly wouldn't let Jack buy my outfit. He has no taste in neckties at all.

CECILY. — I don't think you will require neckties. Uncle Jack is sending you to Australia.

ALGERNON. — Australia! I'd sooner die.

CECILY. — Well, he said at dinner on Wednesday night, that you would have to choose between this world, the next world, and Australia.

ALGERNON. — Oh, well! The accounts I have received of Australia and the next world are not particularly encouraging. This world is good enough for me, cousin Cecily.

CECILY. — Yes, but are you good enough for it?

ALGERNON. — I'm afraid I'm not that. That is why I want you to reform me. You might make that your mission, if you don't mind, cousin Cecily.

CECILY. — I'm afraid I've no time, this afternoon.

ALGERNON. — Well, would you mind my reforming myself this afternoon?

CECILY. — It is rather Quixotic of you. But I think you should try.

ALGERNON. — I will. I feel better already.

CECILY. — You are looking a little worse.

ALGERNON. — That is because I am hungry.

CECILY. — How thoughtless of me! I should have remembered that when one is going to lead an entirely new life, one requires regular and wholesome meals. Won't you come in?

ALGERNON. — Thank you. Might I have a buttonhole first? I never have any appetite unless I have a buttonhole first.

CECILY. — A Maréchal Niel? (*Picks up scissors.*)

ALGERNON. — No, I'd sooner have a pink rose.

CECILY. — Why? (*Cuts a flower.*)

ALGERNON. — Because you are like a pink rose, cousin Cecily.

That dialogue has little resemblance to any earthly conversation between a man and a girl. It is not flirtation as flirtation *appears* to anyone and yet it is the essence of flirtation.

My old friend Mr. Allan Aynesworth, who played the part on the first night and is still very gay and debonair, tells me that, at rehearsals, there were many misgivings about the play. There was a certain hankering after the melodramatic plot, the emotional stress and solemnity which, from the Victorian point of view, had given dramatic substance to Wilde's earlier plays. It was felt, I gather, that *The Importance of Being Earnest* wouldn't give the audience enough to get their teeth into, and that pure froth, pure absurdity, completely without emotion or the slap-stick of Victorian farce, might send them away dissatisfied. It was decided, quite

rightly, never to force a laugh, to speak every line as if the
actor were completely unaware of its being funny; in brief
to rely upon Wilde; but it was decided also to cover his
tracks and at all costs to play quickly and never to be caught
in the trap of waiting for a laugh that didn't come. At a late
rehearsal, which hadn't gone too well, Wilde congratulated
the cast on its good fortune in appearing in a play which
would last as long as English comedy endured, and no one
took him, or believed that he took himself, seriously. Then
a very odd thing happened. On the first night, long before
Lady Bracknell's entrance, as soon as Aynesworth and
Alexander began to play the cucumber-sandwich scene, the
audience began to laugh, and the embarrassing thing was
that they laughed at every line and at almost every phrase of
the longer speeches. The actors were both delighted and dis-
mayed. They had rehearsed the play in one *tempo*; they had,
quite suddenly, to perform it in another; and when the
audience, not content to laugh, interrupted the dialogue with
rounds of applause, they began to understand that they were
engaged in a play which, if laughter ever allowed them to
reach the end of it, would be unique and immortal in the
theatre.

If we can understand why this was so, we shall have come
very near to the innermost secret of comic dialogue. *The
Importance of Being Earnest* owed much of its success to its
superlative good humour, but neither its good humour
nor the delightful impudence of its plot made it a masterpiece. It lives by three things: first that its dialogue, though
it looks like prose, has a formal selectiveness and rhythm;
secondly, that it never for an instant swerves from its own
convention — never in a phrase or a word falters into
solemnity or sentimentality or cruelty or bitterness; and,

finally, that, as a result, it is not merely a pleasant, ingenious, lighthearted play, but carries one, beyond lighthearted behaviour and appearances, into the very essence of lightness of heart.

·    ·    ·    ·

Now, before going any further in the theatre, let us look for a moment at dialogue in the novel. The first thing to notice — because it is a matter of evident fact and not of opinion — is that whereas a play consists wholly of dialogue and visible action, a novel consists of narrative and description, with dialogue used as an auxiliary. The degree in which dialogue is regarded as auxiliary or subordinate differs from novel to novel, and I should not dream of laying down a rule about it; but I think it may be said that a novelist who puts everything or almost everything into direct speech is denying himself many of the richest opportunities of his own craft and is receiving in compensation none of the support given to a dramatist by the stage. In saying this I do not forget that a great masterpiece of our time, *The Dynasts* of Thomas Hardy, was written entirely in dialogue with the intention that it should be read, not acted; but *The Dynasts* is, in effect, not a play and still less a novel; it is an epic poem; and it does not in itself give valid support to those whose novels are an almost uninterrupted patter of talk.

But the real question is not of quantity but of quality and purpose. It seems to me quite certain that the one thing no dialogue must be is microphonic. It must not be, or aim at being, the product of a recording instrument concealed in a bar or at a street-corner or in a drawing-room. There are novels, particularly second-hand, derivative novels written under American influence, which sound very much like that, but do not let us deceive ourselves: the Americans who really write — Faulkner, for example — though they do 'patter' a great deal, are never 'microphonic'. They are not only highly selective but extremely stylized. What gives them their microphonic effect is the fact that they are so often writing about crude and uncultivated men and women who, in life, are loquacious and yet inarticulate. The appetites of these creatures are strong, their opinions stronger, their indignations strongest of all, but in conversation their vocabulary is even smaller than yours and mine and their syntax almost non-existent. Therefore, in conversation, they endlessly stutter and repeat themselves and, in exasperation, shout; or, if they happen not to be hobos, but tycoons, their conversation is a vast sausage-string of polysyllabic clichés, of circumlocutory avoidances. In both cases, the ruling passion is the same — to go on talking and talking in the desperate hope that somehow what they feel so violently will express itself, for unlike the simple folk of Hardy or George Eliot, living in an ancient civilization, the hobos and the tycoons are unaware of their own limitations and have not the once-universal code of Bible imagery to fall back on. It follows that American novelists, when writing on the hobo, the gangster or the tycoon level, have to preserve an appearance of loquaciousness — sometimes as quickfiring as a machine-gun and sometimes a kind of sub-human dribbling — and, at the same time, to express the reality within this appearance: the passionate, the pathetic or the agonized inarticulateness. The conversation itself, if reported microphonically, would be without significance and deadly dull; but the *dialogue* in the hands of an American master, selective and rhythmical, whether we enjoy it or not, is, in its own way, as stylized as the dialogue of Meredith and succeeds for that reason.

I shall not attempt to read an illustrative passage from Faulkner or Hemingway. Everything in their dialogue depends on an intonation and rhythm of which I am incapable. In any case all of you, who are so much younger than I am, are acquainted with these writers; the sound of their tom-toms and their war-cries are sweet and familiar music in your ears, and I shall be content if you will concede that their dialogue at its best is not microphonic but, in its own strange way, poetic and evocative. It would be easy to prove by a reading from the Penny-whistle scene in *The Ordeal of Richard Feverel* that Meredith's dialogue seeks always to discover reality within appearances; it would be easy to make the same point by studying the long cadences of Emily Brontë or the strange resonance — the echo of ghostly footsteps in corridors of bronze — which gives character to the dialogue, as well as to the narrative, of Edgar Allan Poe. We all know that Poe and Meredith and Emily Brontë were poets and I prefer to prove my case from the less obvious examples — from Faulkner and, shall we say, from Defoe.

With Defoe we are at the other end of the story-telling tradition. Defoe saw himself as a naturalist or reporter. His *Journal of the Plague Year* was a kind of naturalist hoax, a piece of fiction designed to give an effect of eye-witness journalism. And Defoe's novel *Moll Flanders* is, above all else, plain-speaking, not high-falutin', not fantasticated, not, in any sense, deliberately stylized. Defoe gave his own definition of a perfect style as 'that in which a man speaking to five hundred people, of all common and various capacities, idiots or lunatics excepted, should be understood by them all and in the same sense which the speaker intended to be understood'. What is the effect of this on Defoe's use of dialogue? It is almost to abolish it. Dialogue if employed at all has to be infused with the author's style; that is why Meredith's characters, while each preserves his or her individuality, all talk Meredith, and Kipling's characters, whether they are private soldiers or acid Anglo-Indian ladies or animals in the jungle, all talk Kipling. This confronted Defoe with a special difficulty. The essence of his style was plainness; his whole strength was in the matter-of-fact. Dialogue, if he used it lavishly, would have had to be matter-of-fact too, and that would have been microphonic, tedious and intolerable. Therefore Defoe used direct speech very rarely. He recounted a great many conversations, but he *recounted* them, using continually the device of indirect speech.

Consider this little scene of love-making:

'I struggled to get away, and yet did it but faintly neither, and he held me fast, and still kissed me, till he was almost out of breath, and then, sitting down, says, "Dear Betty, I am in love with you".

'His words I must confess, fired my blood; all my spirits flew about my heart and put me into disorder enough, which he might easily have seen in my face. He repeated it afterwards several times, that he was in love with me, and my heart spoke as plain as a voice, that I liked it; nay, whenever he said "I am in love with you", my blushes plainly replied, "Would you were, sir".'

Or watch Defoe's treatment when the would-be lover returns to the attack:

'It was his younger sister's chamber that I was in, and as there was nobody in the house but the maids below-stairs, he was, it may be, the ruder; in short, he began to be earnest with me indeed. Perhaps he found me a little too easy, for God knows I made no resistance to him while he only held me in his arms and kissed me; indeed, I was too well pleased with it to resist him much.

'However, as it were, tired with that kind of work, we sat down, and there he talked with me a great while; he said he was charmed with me, and that he could not rest night or day till he had told me how he was in love with me, and, if I was able to love him again, and would make him happy, I should be the saving of his life, and many such fine things. I said little to him again, but easily discovered that I was a fool, and that I did not in the least perceive what he meant.'

In the second passage, though 'he talked with me a great while', there is not a word of direct speech. In the first there are but eight: 'Dear Betty, I am in love with you', and these are deliberately echoed. Thus, by abstaining from dialogue in the special circumstances of his own case, Defoe confirms two principles of dialogue: that, when used, it must harmonize with the writer's style, and, secondly, that its purpose is not to report a conversation but to communicate its essence. Defoe with unerring instinct fastened on the only eight words that really mattered. They were the theme of that conversation; he stated it firmly; he repeated it once; and swept all else away in the swift advance of his own narrative.

I have spoken of Defoe because I wished to illustrate my theme by contrast — the contrast between poetic novelists and the story-teller who is so plainly down-to-earth. It would be pleasant to explore another contrast — that presented by Miss Austen; but that would carry us too far this evening. What is more, in this country, Miss Austen is a kind of religion. It is considered almost blasphemous to do more than call attention to her infallibility, and I have no wish to disturb her congregation at their devotions. It would be the height of indiscretion to criticize the dialogue of a goddess, though I think her worshippers will agree, will indeed claim, that her dialogue also discovers a reality within the appearance of polite manners. It is just a question of whether that reality interests and amuses you, and, if so, in what degree.

.    .    .    .    .

I would add only a word more. The theory of dialogue which I have put forward this evening — that dialogue is not a report but a distillation, a formal means of penetrating to the essence of things — is the theory upon which poetic dialogue rests — and I am speaking now not of dialogue that is poetic only in the wider sense but of dialogue in verse.

It would be foolish to suggest that 'distilled' dialogue, evocative of a reality within appearance, cannot be written in prose, but whoever has attempted it must be aware of two things: first, that the attempt drives him away from naturalism, into non-conversational prose-rhythms heavily charged with poetic overtones; and, secondly, that to strike out clearly into verse would be a relief, a liberation and an enablement. There is, I think, in the dire appearances of contemporary life and in our sense of the spiritual reality underlying those appearances, a new compulsion to write on two planes — the plane of observation and the plane of apprehension — and this compulsion is so strong that it is driving modern dramatic dialogue towards poetry. This you will say is obvious enough, and you will recall with respect and admiration the plays of Mr. Eliot; but if I add that modern dramatic dialogue is being driven towards verse, the question becomes more open, and Mr. Eliot is by no means a final answer to it. I do not wish to enter into a technical argument about Mr. Eliot's prosody. According to certain definitions, he is writing verse, and we will not now dispute those definitions. It is true nevertheless that when he holds his audiences by his intelligence, his feeling, his insight, his story-telling, sometimes even by his rhythm, all these qualities, as he so brilliantly displays them, are far more nearly akin to the qualities of a prose-dramatist with a poet's mind than to those of a poetic dramatist in the ordinary meaning of that phrase.

This of course is, in him, deliberate. Just as in his non-dramatic verse he set out to avoid conventionally poetic language, so, in his plays, he has avoided the classical metres. For all this he had good reasons. It has enabled him to break down barriers in the theatre that might not otherwise have been broken down and to produce work of high distinction. Nevertheless I believe that a greater challenge lies ahead. Dramatic dialogue will not regain its supreme power of distilling human experience and of revealing to ordinary men and women their essence, their being, the innermost truth of their physical and spiritual life, until it enchants them and sings to them and possesses their memories.

The great obstacle is Shakespeare, who has so used and varied the iambic pentameter that any approach to it in the theatre seems now an impudent challenge to his gigantic ghost. And yet a line of ten syllables with five major stresses is the norm of English dramatic dialogue, and I believe we must either use a variant of it or discover an alternative to it that enchants and sings. The other classical English metre — the octosyllables of Andrew Marvell and Rupert Brooke — is too short a line for the theatre, and the line of twelve syllables, though a natural necessity in France, seems not to respond easily to the English genius. Michael Drayton, un-

questionably a great poet and the writer of a sonnet that takes
rank with any of Shakespeare's, chose the twelve-syllable
line for what was to have been his masterpiece, *Poly-
olbion*, and the English ear has rejected it. It is very rarely
that twelve syllables sing to us, and yet sometimes they do.
Once they sang of the essence of things as no poet has ever
sung:

> Then dawns the Invisible, the Unseen its truth reveals;
> My outward sense is gone, my inward essence feels —
> Its wings are almost free, its home, its harbour found;
> Measuring the gulf it stoops and dares the final bound.

But these wonderful verses are rhymed and I greatly doubt
whether it is possible, in an English theatre, to use twelve
syllables blank. We may vary the pentameter as we will and
as we can, just as we may vary the food we eat; but it has
always been the bread and the wine of our poetic life and we
may find in the end that dramatic dialogue cannot do without it. In any case I am certain of one thing: that only a
metre with a basic regularity of stress is able to raise dramatic
dialogue to its highest power. Nothing else can create in an
audience that rhythm of expectation and fulfilment, that
music of the accepting imagination which quiets the petty
uproar of our superficial minds and makes us still and receiving. If, in a play, the President of a People's Republic, about
to be assassinated, were to say in prose: 'Now, boys, sit right
down here and I will tell you why Presidents of People's
Republics are always shot up', no one would be greatly
interested; and even if he were to say in free verse:

> Now, boys, sit right down here and I
> Will tell you why
> Presidents of People's Republics are
> Always shot up

no one would do more than reverently cough. But if the actor were to say:

> For God's sake, let us sit upon the ground
> And tell sad stories of the death of kings,

then, from stalls to gallery, the whole theatre would be hushed and through the stillness of tragedy would sound the music of the Golden World.

Or, if a dramatist wished, at the cold opening of his play, to communicate that a man and woman, whom the audience had not seen before, were passionately in love, how should he do it? It cannot be done in prose. It cannot be done in free verse. But listen:

> CLEOPATRA. — If it be love indeed, tell me how much.
> ANTONY. — There's beggary in the love that can be reckon'd.
> CLEOPATRA. — I'll set a bourn how far to be belov'd.
> ANTONY. — Then must thou needs find out new heaven, new earth.

In four pentameters, all is said. If dialogue is to fly straight to the essence of things, the arrow must sing in the air.

# ON LEARNING TO WRITE *

STYLE, said Professor Walter Raleigh, cannot be taught. It is strictly true; no one by taking pains can become an artist. But it is equally true that no one can be effectively an artist without taking pains. The quality of artist is a gift of the gods granted to a man at birth, a rare and miraculous impregnation. It is increased or diminished in him hour by hour until it bears fruit or dies. Its continuance, like the continuance of all miracles, depends upon his power and will to receive it, and this receptive power depends in its turn upon the artist's fitting himself spiritually to receive the gift of the gods; it is not what we ordinarily mean by a technical process. In this sense, style cannot be taught.

Nevertheless another part of the fructifying process *is* technical and analogous to a husbandman's use of his tools and his care of the ground. This technical part of an artist's life may be learned, and the learning may be carried so far that it ceases to be narrowly technical and becomes a study of the grand strategy of artistic practice. It is with this learning that I am concerned: not only with learning the technical elements of the art of writing but with learning its grand strategy as well, and with both in their relationship to that quality of artist which, if it already exists, they can enable and reveal.

I have said that the technical elements of the art of writing

* Presidential Address to the English Association, 1954.

and its grand strategy can be learned. But can they? We to whom writing has been a life's engagement will say that we studied our craft when we were young and that every day, in our chair and at our desk, we are still trying to learn it. But we did not go, as young painters do, to the Academy Schools or to the Slade; at our universities we read History or English Literature or the Humane Letters, none of which, in the sense now intended, was a direct apprenticeship to our trade; and we find it hard to tell in what the apprenticeship consisted that we claim to have served. How did we begin? How shall we continue? How shall a young man qualify? Is there a writer's apprenticeship at all?

I hope it will not be thought that my choice of subject is pedantic. No one is better aware than I am of the howlers which pedantry may lead men to commit. I once received a rude postcard which ran as follows: 'You who are supposed to be a master of language —' (I am sorry, but I am quoting, and, as you will see, the tribute was ironically intended.)

You who are supposed to be a master of language, what possible authority or excuse can you have for the disgusting American journalese of spelling the word *judgment* with an 'e'?

I replied, also on a postcard:

My authority for what you call American journalese is the Book of Common Prayer.

Silence ensued. Fortunately my angry correspondent did not notice that he had on his side the authority of the Authorized Version. If he had, we might have been exchanging postcards to this day. As it was, I had leisure to reflect that in English there is to be found among the masters authority for almost anything. This adds to the complexity and, I think, to the interest of our subject. We have to ask not only whether there is such a thing as an apprenticeship to the profession of writing but to what masters the apprentice shall devote himself.

2

No one who is untrained would attempt to sing at Covent Garden or dance at Sadler's Wells, but anyone who can hold a pen or chatter to a typist is free to sit down in the cheerful hope of writing a book. Nearly everyone does. If these urgent amateurs are expert in other professions and so are aware that admirals and generals, for example, are made, not born, they sometimes begin by saying modestly that they cannot write, but they are not deterred from taking five hundred pages to illustrate this simple truth. The reason is that, in their heart of hearts, they do not believe it to be true. They think they can write, more or less; and so they can — more or less. That, precisely, is the trouble. To them the idea of there being a profession of writing in the sense in which there is a profession of surgery is unfamiliar and slightly repellent; it is as if one should speak of a professional card-player or a professional charmer. Nor is this surprising. Their little niece Evangeline wrote a best seller last week — and would you believe it, my dear, it's going to be made into a movie? Where was the professionalism in that? Certainly not in Evangeline.

To many minds, the art of writing appears to require no apprenticeship. The reason is, I think, that all other arts have at their root a physical process in which the craftsman must be exercised. They have physical materials or instruments which he must control, and often mathematical rules which he must know how to apply. The art of writing has no

I

corresponding physical or mathematical elements — no laws of perspective or harmony, no scales to play, no legs to kick in the air, and only one trumpet to blow.

The distinction in this respect between the writer's art and all others may be made clear by an anecdote. In my lifelong struggle with words, I have found that to draw has always given me relief and refreshment, and I used at one time to work regularly in the studio of a painter, sharing his models. I worked hard and seriously; was delighted when a drawing succeeded and sad when another failed. At that period of my life I was intimate with George Moore, and my work with him led to friendship with Wilson Steer and Henry Tonks. Tonks was at the end of his mastership at the Slade School. He had a reputation for severity and I was careful to conceal from him my excursions into his own art. George Moore let the cat out of the bag, and I was bidden by a genial Tonks to produce my drawings when next I had supper with him. It was a memorable ordeal. I faced the fire, Tonks on one side, Steer on the other, and my drawings were handed across me from master to master, who argued about them and drew upon them as if I did not exist. Steer was kind enough to say that I was astonishingly accurate, which I took to be all-complimentary until he added: 'Now you must learn to let yourself go. Who is your master — Ingres?' I confessed to an unqualified admiration for Ingres as a draughtsman. 'I thought so,' he said, 'and Ingres is a great master — but there are other masters than Ingres.' Having spoken thus, Steer fell asleep.

Steer had the habits of a dormouse. No evening would have been an evening during which he did not fall asleep. 'I have spent half my life,' George Moore would complain, 'in talking while Steer has slept or in waiting for Lady Cunard.'

Tonks allowed Steer to doze and continued my education independently.

He pinned a sheet of paper to a drawing-board, set up the board firmly on an easel, and put a pencil in my hand. 'Now,' he said, 'draw a straight line.'

Across the middle of the paper, from left to right, I drew from the shoulder what turned out to be a line creditably straight.

'Now,' said Tonks, 'draw the same line from East to West.'

It should have been precisely superimposed upon the first and indistinguishable from it. Alas, it wobbled in the West, but it was an honourable failure. A third line drawn from North to South and bisecting the first two was easier.

'Now,' said the inexorable Tonks, 'let me see you draw a line upwards, from South-east to North-west, through the meeting point of the others — and be careful,' he added with a grim smile, 'that there is no triangle at the middle of the compass.'

So the experiment continued. 'When you can draw straight lines unerringly in any direction and can draw concentric circles clockwise and anticlockwise, then,' said Tonks, 'you will have begun to learn to draw. Without that, all the rest is sham. With it, all the rest becomes at least possible.'

In the process of learning to write there is nothing that corresponds to the drawing of Tonks's straight lines and concentric circles, nothing that is verifiable beyond question by ruler and compass. Our apprenticeship is dangerously vague. We shall come nearer to understanding it if we decide first what is the purpose of apprenticeship in any of the arts and then inquire how that purpose may be attained by a writer.

### 3

The purpose of an apprenticeship, as I understand it, is general not particular. It is to enable a ballet-dancer to dance and an actor to act, to dance or act anything within the range of his physical or mental capacity; it is not to train him to perform a particular part or to confine him within the specialization of a particular school or style. The same is true of the other arts — of music, for example, or of painting: the object of the great teacher is always to lift from his pupil the handicap of technical incapacity, to give him such a control of his tools as may be at least his passport, though not his journey-money, in the voyages he may contemplate. And a great teacher, on condition that he does this, may do more than this. He may give to the pupil historical knowledge of his art, an understanding of its scope and limitations, an awe of its wonders. All this is a legitimate part of apprenticeship because it is an enablement of and a discipline upon the imagination, as Tonks's straight lines were an enablement of and a discipline upon the hand.

An apprenticeship, then, is an enablement through discipline. How is it to be served in the art of writing, which is not based upon a physical process, but upon the selection and ordering of words?

### 4

There is a temptation to answer that a writer must begin by a study of his own elements and that these are grammar, syntax and vocabulary. The answer is tempting to me, for I believe that grammar, syntax and vocabulary are of high importance and I shall return to them. And yet I no more believe that a young Englishman, emerged from school and wishing to write, should begin by an isolated and formal study of them than I believe that Cicero, entering his apprenticeship as a writer, began with *puella, puella, puellam.* He knew by then that, if he loved a girl, he put her inevitably into the accusative case. He knew it, if not by intuition, certainly by ear, and it is, I am sure, by training of the ear that all other elements of a writer's apprenticeship must be ruled. This is by no means to say that his ear is always right or that he is entitled to brush aside grammar and syntax by saying arrogantly, as the heathen do: 'But I don't care for your rules. I write by ear.' My claim is, simply, that, if his ear is wrong, nothing with him can be right, and that therefore his training in the other elements of his craft is dependent upon the training — I stress the word — upon the training of his ear.

It will help him — and help him the more because he is concerned with a living, flexible and changing language — to have a point of reference; to accept in his own mind — though perhaps with a mitigating grain of salt — an absolute authority. Too often this authority is suggested to him by some contemporary enthusiasm or admiration — by admiration of Proust, for example, or of Henry James. Our passionate admirations for our near contemporaries can be extremely fruitful. They are valuable impulses. Just as it is true that a man's life may often trace its flowering to his having fallen under the influence of the right man or the right woman at a moment of stagnation or barrenness, so it is true that an artist's life may owe its harvest to some profound enthusiasm which he afterwards outgrows. But such enthusiasms are seeds or impulses; it is death to invest them with the authority of the Medes and Persians. Proust and Henry James cannot be our law-givers. They are adventurers upon the more recently sprouted branches of our literature and we, if we follow them, shall be left out on the branch. If we are to develop branches of our own, we must return for our authority to the trunk of the everlasting, the everflowering tree.

What is the trunk of the French tree? Frenchmen must answer that. Perhaps Pascal? Perhaps Bossuet? Perhaps, for a more recent perfection, Mérimée? I do not know. I have not a French ear. But I am sure that, for an Englishman, the Authorized Version of the Bible and a great part of the Book of Common Prayer — particularly the Litany — may well serve as an absolute authority, a point of reference for grammar, syntax and ear.

Here, then, is a preliminary answer to the student's question: to what master shall I go? You go to the Authorized Version. If you read it and hear it read aloud day after day and night after night, your ear will become so experienced in the splendour and sweetness of our language that it will intuitively reject vulgarism. You may not in consequence write great prose; but at least you will have a vocabulary; you will have grasped that the first principle of narrative is movement; of description, lucidity; of drama, conflict; of vision, attack. This is to make some advance in your apprenticeship.

5

The Bible, like Shakespeare, can lead a grammarian into trouble. Many, including Fowler, have pointed out that, in the third scene of the third act of *The Tempest*, 'Young Ferdinand, *whom* they suppose is drown'd', has not an academic leg to stand on. That does not disturb me. Shakespeare is a volcano, and scholarship, I am glad to say, will never succeed in calling him to order. It was, I think,

Chateaubriand who said something to the effect that Napoleon knew little about generalship except how to win battles. It sounds absurd. Flaubert thought it so, and pilloried Chateaubriand for having written it. But is it as stupid as Flaubert supposed? It is possible to be a transcendent genius in war without being a pattern of generalship. Napoleon's campaign of 1814 makes Chateaubriand's judgement look foolish. It was, even technically, a masterpiece, but all Napoleon's victories were not. They were often attended by that element of so-called 'luck' which attends only supreme genius and cannot be learnt. This, I suppose, is what Chateaubriand meant.

What he said of Napoleon might almost be repeated of Shakespeare in his own turbulent and golden world. The battle-scenes in *Antony and Cleopatra* are, as Godfrey Tearle once said to me, structurally a mess, and yet to what a victory of genius they lead! Whether Shakespeare says 'who' or 'whom' is not relevant; he is a point of reference for devils and angels, not for apprentices. The Authorized Version is another matter. It is written, tactically and strategically, in such a way that we can base ourselves on it as we certainly cannot base ourselves on the Shakespearian volcano.

Having now rashly blotted my Shakespearian copy-book, I await without alarm the onslaught of biblical grammarians. One will challenge me to defend Matthew xviii. 12.

How think ye? if a man have an hundred sheep, and one of them be gone astray, doth he not leave the ninety and nine, and *goeth* into the mountains, and *seeketh* that which is gone astray?

That 'goeth' and 'seeketh' cannot be defended. The Authorized translators must have adjourned for luncheon in mid-sentence. They do not repeat their error when the sheep strays again in Luke xv. 4. The Revisers say:

doth he not leave the ninety and nine, and *go* into the mountains, and *seek* . . .

and the Revisers are, on this occasion, right.

'What about Matthew xvi. 15?' That notorious blunder was the origin in me of a recurring nightmare. In my dream a small boy brought me an essay in which he had written: 'I saw a man in the field. Whom do you think he was?' I crossed out the *m* of 'whom' and sent the boy to the bottom of the class, in which humiliating position he raised his hand and his voice and said 'What about Matthew xvi. 15? "But whom say ye that I am?"' And in my dream I put sack-cloth upon my head. But one night, I thought of the answer. When the lamentable brat raised his hand and his voice and quoted my own absolute Authority against me, I answered him, saying: 'Child, thou art justified; go thou to the top of the class. But don't do it again. And write out the Revised Version forty times save one.' He must still be writing it, for I have not seen him again.

I return then to the Authorized Version with unshaken confidence. My claim is not that we should restrict ourselves to it. The language has changed since then and we are entitled, we are bound, to recognize the change. The neuter possessive pronoun 'its' does not occur in the Authorized Version, but Shakespeare was beginning to use it — he used it ten times, I believe — and though it is a nasty, hissing word, still to be avoided in speaking of the sun or the moon or a ship, we cannot now do without it.

There is much else that we may say and write for which the Bible does not give authority, and there are many of its uses — for example the use of the second person singular —

that are denied to us. Let us say only, as we learn our trade: 'This book is a standard to which we must refer and from which we may diverge — if we have reason enough. But we will not diverge ignorantly or incompetently or without balancing the gain against the loss.'

Those who speak with legitimate pride of the vitality of our language and of the recent extensions of our vocabulary often forget what a price has been paid in the death of good words and beautiful inflexions. The loss of the second person singular, whatever the compensations for it may be, is in itself an impoverishment of English, just as the virtual abandonment of the imperfect subjunctive is an impoverishment of French. I am not pleading for their restoration, but it seems wise that a student of writing, while accepting a new usage, should at least not be ignorant of the old, and should be aware, as he will be if he is familiar with the Authorized Version, of the price that he may have to pay. And, what is more, he will find that the Authorized Version can be not only a preservative but a liberating influence. Have we not all argued with ourselves about the use of 'which' or 'that' as a relative pronoun? For many years, because I love a variety of language that precisely corresponds to a variety of meaning, I tried to preserve a distinction between 'which' and 'that' that marked — or which marked — a distinction of meaning. I still try, but it is not easy. And it is a relief to find that the Authorized Version over-rules my endeavour and allows 'which' and 'that' to be interchangeable. In the sentence beginning: 'Render therefore unto Caesar . . .' (Matthew xxii. 21) there are two relative clauses; neither is more defining or more informative than the other; the resemblance between them is complete and precise. And yet the translators introduce the first with 'which' and the second with 'that'. 'Render therefore unto Caesar the things *which* are Caesar's and unto God the things *that* are God's.' The Revisers have preferred to be consistent; they use 'that' twice. I hold to the freedom of the Authorized Version. It is a perfect example of the truth that, in the application of rules, the final court of appeal is ear.

Another good reason for accepting the Bible and the Prayer Book as basic authorities is that they are — or were until a few years ago — current. This cannot be claimed in the same degree for any other books as old, even for Shakespeare, who, in any case, is not an authority for prose. Shakespeare's great Queen is a prose-authority whom I should dearly love to accept, and indeed for writers with the disease of woolliness she is strong medicine. Listen to her reply of 10 April 1563 (D'Ewes's *Journals*, 75–81) when Parliament had urged her to marry and safeguard the succession:

. . . Since there can be no duer debt than princes' words, which I would observe, therefore I answer to the same. Thus it is; the two petitions which you made unto me do contain two things, my Marriage, and Succession after me. For the first, if I had let slip too much time, or if my strength had been decayed, you might the better have spoke therein; or if any think I never meant to try that life, they be deceived; but if I may hereafter bend my mind thereunto, the rather for fulfilling your request, I shall be therewith very well content. For the second, the greatness thereof maketh me to say and pray, that I may linger here in this vale of misery for your comfort, wherein I have witness of my study and travail for your surety: and I cannot, with 'nunc dimittis', end my life, without I see some foundation of your surety after my gravestone.

And listen again to her reply (D'Ewes's *Journals*, 380–402) when Parliament, in 1586, had come howling to her, not once but twice, for the blood of the Scottish Queen:

If I should say unto you that I mean not to grant your petition, by my faith I should say unto you more than perhaps I mean. And if I should say unto you I mean to grant your petition, I should then tell you more than is fit for you to know. And thus I must deliver you an answer answerless.

To young ladies who cannot say No, or have not courage or authority enough to reserve judgement to themselves, I commend these passages as a text to hang above their virgin beds. And yet Shakespeare's Queen is not the general authority to which a modern writer may look, for the antique in her is not brought close to us, as the Bible and the Prayer Book are, by the familiarity of our mother's knee.

The familiarity of the Bible and the Prayer Book is now declining. So much the worse for us. How much the worse may be clearly seen if we compare the petitions and prayers, written by living hands, which are sometimes used in churches on special occasions, with the words of the Prayer Book itself. Even in our prayers we are timidly hesitant as though we were candidates at an election-meeting anxious to compromise, to conciliate all comers, and, therefore, not to commit ourselves. Who now would have the courage to open with: 'Stir up, we beseech thee, O Lord, the wills of thy faithful people. . . .'? Or who would dare to write: 'That it may please thee to strengthen such as do stand; and to comfort and help the weak-hearted; and to raise up them that fall; and finally to beat down Satan under our feet'? 'To *beat down Sa*tan . . .' — where, except in Churchill at war, shall we find the passionate energy that can drive a stress on to three consecutive syllables? We are half-afraid of emphasis as we are half-afraid of poetry. 'Lighten our darkness, we beseech thee, O Lord; and by thy great mercy defend us from all perils and dangers of this night. . . .' If you or I were given the grace to write that, some astringent compromiser would object to it as rhetorical and sentimental, and say that 'perils and dangers' was repetitive. Finally, let those who write of the kidnapping and the mock-trials of brave men behind the Iron Curtain, consider this:

And they stirred up the people, and the elders, and the scribes, and came upon him, and caught him, and brought him to the council, And set up false witnesses, which said, This man ceaseth not to speak blasphemous words against this holy place, and the law: For we have heard him say, that this Jesus of Nazareth shall destroy this place, and shall change the customs which Moses delivered us. And all that sat in the council, looking stedfastly on him, saw his face as it had been the face of an angel. (Acts vi. 12–15.)

That goes to the very root of narrative.

From the Prayer Book and the Bible we English may learn how to pray and how to tell a story, where to begin, how to end, how to orchestrate, how to be simple and direct. These things are the armoury of writers.

6

'Yes,' you will say, 'but a writer must learn how to adapt his arms and use them in the modern world. How shall he do this?'

I should have liked to answer, in the first place: 'by the study of Greek and Latin', but, though I believe the answer to be true, it is not one that I am entitled to make. Having become a naval officer before I entered my 'teens, I spent my youth in a riot of mechanics, physics, chemistry, seamanship, navigation, history, English, French — an extremely civilized and liberal education, if I may say so, but not a classical one. It was not until my twenty-first year that, wishing to go to Oxford, where at that time Greek and Latin

guarded the gate, I withdrew with a tutor into deep country
and set about taming the two monsters. I had three and a
half months before my exam, and I started from scratch: that
is to say, in Greek, with mysterious signs called alpha, beta,
gamma, and, in Latin, with such knowledge of *puella*,
*puella*, *puellam* as had not escaped me since I left my pre-
paratory school at the innocent age of twelve. It was a race
against time, but, believe me, when you are twenty and have
been dreaming of Oxford in the Atlantic and the China Seas,
when you are Jude the Obscure suddenly given his chance,
you can learn anything in three and a half months. At the
end of that breathless and enchanted time I bicycled in over
Magdalen Bridge to my exam, and the two monsters — they
had become goddesses by then — let me pass. It was an
ironic miracle. In a few weeks war broke out; I was a naval
officer again; and though, some five years later, I came to
Oxford at last, the classical goddesses had departed from
me. I have never ceased to be aware of my loss. Not to be
able to read Plato in the original; not to be able to listen
while Catullus sings; not to be able to hear (apart from the
rule) why *Tempora mutantur nos et mutamur in illis* is good
and why *et nos* makes it vile — is a perpetual handicap.
Greek and Latin teach an Englishman what it is hard for him
to learn otherwise — case, mood, tense, voice and a thousand refinements different from his own; but they teach him
much more — a reverence for language itself, an active sense
of the limitations of each language, so that while he fights his
own battle for an elusive meaning he may be fortified against
the accursed blight of 'It couldn't matter less' by the sound
and memory of battles long ago.

My lack of scholarship deprives me of the right to commend classical learning to others, but it does not forbid me

to say that, as a learner of English — and indeed as a learner of life —, I have felt the absence of Greek and Latin in me as a kind of maiming. It is as though I were going about the world half-deaf.

## 7

However, we must do our best with what equipment we have. A great and increasing part of the world suffers from my disability in the classics, and yet we must learn to write. Two things are chiefly necessary: self-exercise, and a study of the right masters in the right way.

After the Bible and the Prayer Book, who are the 'right' masters? Not necessarily those by whom we are most deeply moved. If that were the test, my teacher should have been Emily Brontë, for her novel, more than any other in the world, makes my heart turn over. If that were the test, then, among the Russians, my early master should have been Dostoevski, but do not let us forget what Tolstoy said on that subject. It is a passage which I have quoted before, but it is worth recalling. In writing to Strakhov, Dostoevski's biographer, Tolstoy said:

I have read your book. . . . He is touching and interesting, but one cannot set on a pedestal for the instruction of posterity a man who was all struggle. From your book I have learnt for the first time the whole measure of his mind. Pressensé's book I have also read, but all his learning is spoilt by a flaw. There are beautiful horses: but if a trotter, worth, say 1000 rubles, suddenly proves restive, then — beautiful and strong as it is — it is worthless. The longer I live, the more I value horses that are not restive. You say that you are reconciled to Turgenev. And I have come to love him very much; and, curiously enough, just because he is not restive but gets to his destination — not like a trotter that will not take one to the journey's end and may even land one in a ditch. But Pressensé and Dostoevski are both restive; and so all the erudition of the one and the wisdom and heart of the other run to waste. Turgenev will outlive Dostoevski, and not for his artistic qualities but because he is not restive. . . .

'Restive' is a key-word. George Moore raised a corresponding objection to Emily Brontë — 'Ah, she is too wuthering!' — an exclamation which infuriated me as a general assault upon my goddess but which is of value in our present context. The great visionaries open our eyes; they enable an artist to see, and keep alive within him his own original fire; but if they are 'restive' or if their power depends, as Emily Brontë's did, not upon the virtues that may be learned and shared but upon a unique quality of incantation, they can do little to remove the technical disabilities of men learning to write and may, indeed, increase them.

For the same reason, the eccentrics — Carlyle or Peacock — are dangerous masters. Even a mature writer, firm in his own technique, knows that there are certain books he must not read before sitting down to his own work. They may be books of the highest rank, but for him, at that moment, they are too violent or too mannered, too highly flavoured or too highly scented. If one has been reading Carlyle or Peacock or Pater or — shall we say? — *The New Yorker*, one must give oneself time, before beginning to write, to get the rhythm out of one's mind and the taste out of one's mouth. This is not to disparage the rhythm or the taste. It is to say only that for the purposes of learning how to write we do better to study — I will not say the 'plainer' masters, for that word might seem to exclude Gibbon — but those masters whose merit, like Goldsmith's, greatly depends on the firmness of their line, the lucidity of their expression, and their use of form, not primarily to decorate their page or to charm or astonish their readers — but as a means of fully communicating and lighting their intention.

These certainly are among the merits of the Authorized Version. They are among the merits of writers as different in other ways as Goldsmith and Gibbon. They are the merits of what I dare to call the direct inheritance — the inheritance, from the Bible, of Milton and Jeremy Taylor, of Defoe, Addison, Steele and Fielding, but not, in the same degree, of Sterne or Smollett or Beckford who, each in his own way, stands a little aside. So does De Quincey, splendid though he is, stand aside as too often preferring, like Francis Thompson in our own age, the decoration to the architecture of prose. For our purpose, Hazlitt is the master in De Quincey's time, or, if we will have a giant to teach us, Landor. There are, no doubt, some who think Landor too stately. Very well; it may be that his is a bow that we cannot draw. Nevertheless, may we not learn from him that there were arrows once? Landor, moreover, was not as antique as some, who have not studied him, believe. He knew all there is to know about the delaying cadence which, in deference to Henry James, it is now fashionable to cultivate. Henry James is celebrated as a master of the delaying cadence which, by holding up a sentence with qualifications and refinements, brilliantly intensifies meaning by suspending it. For this quest of precision the later Henry James is justly praised, but those who imitate him too piously and are in danger of catching his stutter without achieving his flashes of lucidity might profit by observing that delay and suspense were not his invention, and that their use need not be accompanied by an impediment of speech. Here is Henry James (*The Art of the Novel*, 281):

Only then, as he's quite liable to say to himself, what would perhaps become, under the dead collective weight of those knowledges that he may, as the case stands for him, often separately miss, what would become of the free intensity of the perceptions which serve him in their stead, in which he never hesitates to rejoice, and to which, in a hundred connexions, he just impudently trusts?

Read it three times and its meaning all-subtly and quite beautifully does, as it were, perhaps, emerge. Compare Landor's account of Aspasia at the theatre:

I will now tell you all. No time was to be lost, so I hastened on shore in the dress of an Athenian boy, who came over with his mother from Lemnos. In the giddiness of youth he forgot to tell me that, not being yet eighteen years old, he could not be admitted and he left me on the steps. My heart sank within me, so many young men stared and whispered; yet never was stranger treated with more civility. Crowded as the theatre was (for the tragedy had begun), every one made room for me. When they were seated, and I too, I looked toward the stage; and behold there lay before me, but afar off, bound upon a rock, a more majestic form, and bearing a countenance more heroic, I should rather say more divine, than ever my imagination had conceived.

Observe the delays of that last sentence. They obscure nothing; they do not discourage the reader but enchant him; they are, in themselves, a source of melody as are the little rocks and pebbles that check a stream but do not choke it. I am persuaded that Landor is a master of great value to us because, impatient though he was as a man, his approach to language is so nobly clear, patient and loving. He is in the direct inheritance which we may follow down to Thackeray and beyond.

The principle is always the same — that meaning is a goddess to be wooed, not raped. She cannot be won by tricks. She is to be wooed with all the resources of language and with an ardour governed by form. She will not yield herself to violence, but only to those who study how to know her and lead her out. Henry James, heaven knows,

K

was not violent. His courtship was elaborate and devoted. He was an untiring perfectionist and experimentalist; as such we honour him and, if I may put it so, sit at the feet of his difficulties. Nevertheless, if we would learn to write, we must, I think, look first to the steadfast masters who, in Tolstoy's meaning of the word, are not 'restive', and who, in the painter's phrase, 'know how to draw'.

## 8

We come then to the final problem of self-exercise. I believe that a young writer should avoid, at the outset, a high degree of specialization within his own art. He should not begin by saying to himself: 'I am a naturalist' or 'I am a disciple of So-and-So' or 'I am a candidate for membership of Tommy's group or Harry's coterie'. To do this is to make himself exclusive, and it is the essential quality of his apprenticeship, as I understand it, that it be liberal. He is, then, to exercise himself in all kinds of writing and to seek rather than avoid external restriction and compulsion.

The pressure of a great newspaper — its limitations of space and time, its rule against subjective extravagance, its requirement of lucidity, the sense of responsibility with which it inspires those to whom it lends its authority — is an invaluable discipline. One does not write slackly or with self-indulgence when the machines of Printing House Square are muttering in one's ears. One goes in each night with a determination to write, *within the limits of the selected medium*, better than one has ever written before. And that is more than half the battle.

But every young writer has not the good fortune to be harnessed by a great newspaper. He must then harness himself, and the harness consists in his willingness not to be 'restive' but to work within the limits of the medium appropriate to his subject. He will learn from Kipling and Tchekov the difference between a short story and a sketch; he will practise both and despise neither. He will learn from Defoe how to write a novel almost without dialogue and how, by the selection rather than the accumulation of evidence, to create an illusion in the reader's mind that he is listening to an eye-witness. He will learn from Turgenev, and in a different way, from Thackeray, that the oblique method of narration is not the only one. If what you are concerned with is to advance the present action and you reach a point at which the appearance of a new character makes retrospect desirable, two courses lie open. Either you may say: 'I must not appear to be giving information; therefore, at the risk of entanglement, I will imply the past by a series of hints' — and this method, almost inevitable in the theatre where the advance of the visible action must be maintained, is to be studied in Ibsen's inductions. Or you may say with Turgenev: 'But this is a novel, not a play. For the sake of lucidity and speed, I will turn back and tell the reader about the newly arrived character. That done, I shall advance the more easily.' A young writer, who is not hoodwinked by the oblique fashion, will observe that the two methods exist. He will exercise himself in both and will choose between them.

In all his work, not only at the beginning but to the end of his life, he may, I think, find it useful to impose upon himself, particularly in his shorter pieces, a limitation of space. 'This piece,' he may say before he begins, 'shall be so long and no longer.' He will then deliberately write more — perhaps twenty per cent more — and cut. I do not mean that he will cut in chunks. He will cut in sentences, phrases, single words, until, in an athlete's metaphor, his prose is 'trained down' and is fighting-fit. This is the converse of Balzac's method of covering the whole ground shortly, and building up and amplifying in the huge margins of many proofs.

The process of training-down, of cutting, will be painful, but it will teach a writer two things: the tactical lesson of how to rid his prose of superfluous flesh, and at least a part of the great strategical lesson of how to estimate more and more accurately the true relationship between subject and treatment. Is the story I have in mind to be compressed to the length of Turgenev's *Mumu*? Is it a short novel with the range of his *Torrents of Spring* or *First Love*? Does its more complex structure require, and will it sustain, the greater length of *Virgin Soil*? That is one point of view. The other, the point of view of a looser stylist than Turgenev, suggests a different question. Have I here a subject rich and broad and varied and profound enough to justify me in using the looser treatment — the treatment of a far-ranging giant — used by Dostoevski in *The Brothers Karamazov* or by Dickens in *Bleak House*? The two points of view — that of a story seeking its treatment and that of a style seeking its story — have to be reconciled. When a bad book is written by a great writer the reason is nearly always that he has chosen a subject which, however good in itself, is wrong for him. And lesser writers make the same mistake. We have to learn not to make it and I am inclined to think that the elementary process of writing too long and cutting is a first step towards a just reconciliation of subject and treatment.

Another problem that apprenticeship may help us to understand is that of attack. Walkley, who preceded me as dramatic critic of *The Times*, taught me that in a theatre-

notice, particularly in a theatre-notice written to the sound
of a ticking clock, the first sentence is all-important. It sets
the tone and governs the structure of what follows. This is
true, in principle, of all writing. Consider the novel, and
characterization within a novel. Every story and the life of
every character may be spoken of — for the purposes of
illustration — as running from A to Z. The question is: 'At
what point do I plunge in?' If I begin early — perhaps at
point D — my progress from D onward is eased because I
carry no heavy burden of retrospect. On the other hand, if
the crisis of my narrative is late — perhaps at point R — I
may well be guilty of over-prolonging my approach to it if
I start at point D; the story will then sag between D and R.
The alternative is to plunge in much later, perhaps at M, to
shorten the approach MR, and to face, during that approach,
the task of carrying the long retrospect AM. The burden of
long retrospect is made particularly difficult in English by
the troubles of our pluperfect. The word 'had' is not a
pretty one; the two words 'had had', taken together, are a
rock that we must sail many miles to avoid. Whoever studies
the gigantic retrospect at the opening of George Moore's
*The Lake* will observe how often and with how much skill
he avoids shipwreck. Here he accepted all the risks of late
entry. Each of us must decide which of the two sets of risks
he will accept, and his choice will be governed by the nature
of his story and by his self-critical knowledge of his own
weakness and strength. The difficulty of choice is extreme —
even more difficult than the choice between first-person narrative, third-person narrative restricted to the view of a
single character and third-person narrative in which the
author permits himself the all-embracing, all-penetrating
view of the immortal gods. One thing is certain — that

though these choices may now and then be made rightly, as they were by Emily Brontë, with the unselfconscious intuition of genius, they are ordinarily made wrongly, as they were in the case of her sister Anne, by an inexperienced mind. *The Tenant of Wildfell Hall* is an illuminating instance. The early part of it is of the first rank; indeed, Moore would say, perhaps a little wilfully, that it was better than anything else written by a woman; but the later part, as he admitted, falls to pieces, and it falls to pieces because Anne did not know how to make the technical distinctions and choices which we have been discussing.

I shall no doubt be told by those to whom genius and amateurism are equivalent that I have insisted overmuch upon the professional aspects of a writer's art. Or I shall be told that a writer's aestheticism and the practical application of his aestheticism are of no consequence; that only his ideology matters. I hold and shall continue to hold until I die an opposite view. I believe that there are young writers who may not altogether reject or despise the counsel of a fellow learner older than themselves and may indeed value it the more because it has not been vague, but technical and concrete.

I would add one word more. The centre, the core, the essence of all our learning is the power to communicate. Lucidity is by no means all, but it is the virtue 'without which not'. The mark of a charlatan is that he does not try to be lucid — not that he sometimes fails. A writer may fail with certain subjects before certain audiences because they are incapable of receiving what he has to give. The failure, then, is not his but theirs. He is not to write down to them. But let him examine himself. Let him not say, even if he be a mystic: 'I am above the battle. If I am not understood, the fault is not mine'. That is charlatanism and arrogance. The resources of language are great; let him use them all, let him bend himself to be clear. Emily Brontë and Verlaine in *Sagesse* described the mystic's experience with absolute lucidity. It is not impossible to genius, but it would be impossible even to genius that did not care to be lucid. The nobler an artist's inspiration, the more remote and difficult his subject, the more necessary is it that he clear the wires. Only the little men with nothing to say can afford not to learn to write.

# TROLLOPE'S *AUTOBIOGRAPHY*

THE *Autobiography* of Trollope has enduring value as an indirect revelation of a lovable man and of the mid-Victorian age in which he lived. It has, too, what may be called a recurrent value as a mirror in which each new school of literary taste may examine its own features. When the book first appeared, the Aesthetic Movement was in the flood of its reforming enthusiasm, and, like other movements in that state, was extremely intolerant of its immediate predecessors. The result was a violent collapse after Trollope's death of a reputation that had already declined during his later years, and a period of contemptuous neglect which even those who do not call themselves Trollopians now recognize as having been unjust. Since then, time has had its revenge, as it always has upon literary cliques. The aesthetic writers in their turn have been ostracized by the apostles of 'starkness' and 'social consciousness'; it has been fashionable to speak scornfully of them all, from Walter Pater to George Moore; and even Matthew Arnold's *Essays in Criticism*, which do not belong to the Aesthetic Movement, have until very lately been treated, because their approach to art was primarily aesthetic, as being irrelevant to modern judgement. A later group, called the Georgians, among whom Brooke, Flecker and Nichols were conspicuous, has suffered a like fate. Having flowered in the second decade of the twentieth century, these poets were trodden down in the third and fourth with the same ferocious prejudice as was visited upon Trollope in the eighties and nineties.

To anyone who can praise Shelley without damning Pope or who can acknowledge the virtue of Whitman's free verse without despising Gray's *Elegy* as old-fashioned, this traffic of the coteries, so like the shunting of suburban trains in and out of a terminal railway-station, may not seem a good cause for hatred or the hanging-out of revolutionary flags; but we have to recognize it as one of the ways in which literature works out its destiny by a process of selection, wasteful and clumsy though that process may seem to be, and not complain about the latest folly of the latest enthusiast any more than we complain when our daughters fall in and out of love. They will marry in the end, bear children and die; the race will continue, the fittest will survive, and the passionate preference of last Tuesday morning be forgotten. So will the extravagant hatred and the equally extravagant exaltation of Trollope be forgotten, and he will quietly endure, or fail to endure, on his merits as a storyteller. Avowed Trollopians will cease to worship and anti-Trollopians to denigrate him. Indeed they are already ceasing. Trollope is no longer a party-feud. His reputation is settling down, and a reader of his *Autobiography* may enjoy it for its own sake and take of its writer a calm, steady view not, perhaps, greatly different from the view that men will take a hundred years hence. Trollope, in brief, is almost, though not quite, in his niche. Future generations, intent upon their own affairs and ordinarily indifferent to his, will glance in his direction now and then. He will be mentioned in the text-books, and sometimes one or two of his many volumes will be read. The question is — which will be read and with how much respect or affection? There is good reason to believe that the *Autobiography* may be among its writer's principal titles to such immortality as is accorded to him.

It was written, like everything else of his, as part of a laborious routine, but, unlike everything else, without a view to immediate publication. During 1875 he went to Australia, finishing *Is He Popenjoy?* on 3rd May at sea. Having reached Australia in early June, he began at once another book, *The American Senator*, and finished it on 24th September during his return voyage. When he came home, the state of his production was this: *The Way We Live Now* (two volumes) had been published in July; *The Prime Minister* (four volumes) was about to appear in monthly numbers; and the two books finished at sea, which together would make up six volumes, were in reserve. Even Trollope may not unreasonably have thought that the demands of the press upon him were not urgent. During that winter the indefatigable man hunted more than ever, buying fresh horses and 'always trying to resolve that I would give it up', and occupied his writing hours in what one likes to think was almost the recreation of his *Autobiography*. It occupied him for seven months — a leisurely pace for Trollope — and was finished on 30th April, within a week of his sixty-first birthday. Then, as if he had loitered too long, he allowed himself one day off and began another three volumes, *The Duke's Children*, on 2nd May.

When his *Autobiography* was done, Trollope had rather less than seven years to live. He died on 6th December 1882, and the *Autobiography* appeared in the following year. It was condemned because in it he made no claim to inspiration or genius, acknowledging without shame, and indeed with pride, that he wrote for so many hours a day and counted upon producing so many words an hour. He was extremely interested in the money paid for those words, and in 1879 added to his *Autobiography* a table showing that his forty-five books had, with 'sundries', earned for him £68,939 17s. 6d. It was a great sum even then; a modern author, having made allowance for taxation and the increased cost of living, would have to earn roughly half-a-million pounds in order to enjoy an equivalent purchasing power; * but it was not Trollope's success that offended his opponents so much as the laborious means by which he had attained it. When he began a book, he prepared a diary or plan, decided when the book should be finished, and assigned to himself, as a regular task, so many words a week. The lowest assignment was 5000, the highest 28,000, and the average 10,000. A reader, who is unaccustomed to reckon in words, may be assured that this output of imaginative writing is prodigious. Trollope accomplished it while performing steadily his work at the Post Office and pursuing the other activities of his life. The years 1867 and 1868 were, he tells us, his busiest. He had left the Post Office but still had been partly employed by it. He had established the *St. Paul's Magazine*, had stood unsuccessfully for Parliament, had hunted three days a week and had written five novels. No one who has not been a novelist and at the same time carried the burden of another task can fully understand how wonderful was Trollope's energy or how firm and courageous his mind. His immediate successors, to some of whom irregularity of life and

---

* The calculation is very rough and requires a Trollopian footnote. In order to enjoy Trollope's income after deduction of tax a modern writer would have to earn three times as much as he. The tax-free residue would buy three-sevenths of what it bought for Trollope. I have therefore multiplied his seventy thousand first by three, then by seven over three. This gives approximately half-a-million.

'bohemianism' appeared as a necessary part of genius, loathed him for his virtues and, even more, for that pride in them which they regarded as dull-minded complacency. They assumed that books produced as he produced his could not be works of art. Nor, by the aesthetic definition, were they. Within the area of the aesthetic creed, the hostile critics of Trollope were justified; he never wrote an aesthetic novel nor, I would venture to add, a profoundly imaginative one. But his critics were wrong in condemning him on the ground that his approach to life and art was different from theirs. They failed, as every exclusive coterie fails, to observe that the aesthetic truth which they saw, though true enough, was not the whole truth. No theory of art or of life represents the whole truth; but each coterie and sect assumes that its own theory is a final orthodoxy, and so, in time, is made ridiculous.

Trollope has suffered a strange fate from the sects — being damned in the eighties as commercial and complacent, and as extravagantly belauded some fifty years later as a paragon of perfection. In fact, as a careful reader of his *Autobiography* or of any of his novels will see, he was neither a thick-skinned dullard nor, in any reasonable critical sense, perfect. He was a hasty and often a clumsy writer. His prose is neither elegant, enchanting nor evocative. He is poor in fantasy; his imagination, though powerful as a spur to his study of character, is wingless, it never leaves the earth — and that, precisely, is where his strength lies: in the firmness of his feet on earth, in the strength and regularity of their tread; in the sense, which the reader has always, that no tricks are being played on him, that the author is not satirizing what he seems to praise or despising what he depicts as admirable, and that he is trying above all else to do two things: to tell the truth about those aspects of men that interest him, and, in telling it, to be 'readable'. Trollope has many limitations but, within them, he is the least spurious of writers; he never outreaches his own genuine interest; he is sentimental but not high-falutin'; he rides his own hunters without pretending that he keeps Pegasus in his stables.

His *Autobiography* unfailingly gives this impression. Mr. Michael Sadleir, who has done more than anyone else to win back for Trollope the place he deserves, speaks of it as 'this queer bleak text-book of the mechanics and economics of novel-writing', and it is in this queerness and bleakness that Trollope's strange power of not falsifying anything is made manifest. His account of his suffering childhood and youth is neither self-pitying nor a deliberately brave avoidance of self-pity. His account of his success is equally candid, being given in terms of those things which genuinely pleased him — money, comfort, the pleasant sense of being someone, the joy he had in his popularity at the Garrick Club, above all his satisfaction in working hard and competently. The truth seems to be that though, in his early years, Trollope was without self-confidence, he gained it as the years passed. In this gain, and in the visible and tangible evidence of it, he was happy — or as happy as an inwardly diffident man can ever be. He did not count his money because he was a miser, or his words because he confused quality with quantity. He counted both because he had once been afraid of life and because every thousand pounds earned and every day's work punctually accomplished told him — what he most needed to be told — that he was not a failure. He did not step beyond the limits of what he thought it proper to tell and these limits were, by Rousseau's standards, narrow, but a reader would be uncommonly insensitive who, while reading 'this queer bleak text-book', did not grasp that it was abnormally true, and feel himself to be in the presence of a genial, blunt, boisterous man within whom resided always a surprised and alarmed gratitude for whatever good the world yielded him. Trollope was not content to be supinely grateful; he hunted that good seven days a week. To him success was both a reassurance and a sport, and he did not hesitate to say so.

.    .    .    .

The Trollopian veracity is like no other veracity. It is by no means a simple product of a desire to tell the truth, and even less of a Rousseau-like determination to tell the whole truth — that was far from Trollope's polite design. It springs from his limitations as well as from his honesty, from his negative as well as from his positive qualities; it is both deliberate, because he was pugnacious, and involuntary, because he was ingenuous as so many of the solid Victorians were ingenuous; and veracity was, so to speak, squeezed out of him by the conflicting pressures of his nature. The point is that, unlike the veracity sought by the Realists, his was neither cultivated nor exhibitionistic; it was a part of himself, of his extremely restricted self, and therefore a part of his style.

It is to be expected, then, that it should appear in his novels as well as in his *Autobiography*, but the effect, in the two instances, is different. In spite of an undeniable artificiality of contrivance and, sometimes, a plodding heaviness of treatment, the novels are saved from the charge, to which the work of so many of his contemporaries lies open, of being spurious. Trollope, like the rest, wrote for the then almighty circulating libraries; he conformed as dutifully as any to the negative demands of his public, and when, in *The Vicar of Bullhampton*, his object was to 'excite not only pity but sympathy with a fallen woman', he did so with extreme caution and, in a preface reprinted in his *Autobiography*, gave a defensive answer to the question 'whether a novelist, who professes to write for the amusement of the young of both sexes, should allow himself to bring upon his stage a character such as that of Carry Brattle'. What an opportunity for his enemies in 1883! The single admission that he professed to write for the amusement of the young of both sexes was enough to condemn him as both trivial and hypocritical. And yet Trollope was neither, for the good reason that the limitations imposed by the circulating libraries upon fiction closely corresponded with the limitations imposed upon it by his own taste and by what he would have called 'manliness'. The circulating-library readers (when they read fiction, though not always on other occasions) wished to see the world between blinkers and they happened to be the blinkers which suited Trollope. He did not wish to look round them; so little did he wish to look round them that he seems not to have grasped how Thackeray, his adored master, was tormented and quickened by a desire to do so. Nor was he capable of penetrating deeply into what he did see. But, between his blinkers, he observed the conduct, the manners, the pretences and the honesties of men and women accurately, and, accepting the good and the bad with a shrug, had no impulse to falsify his report. So it has happened that he, who was in many respects a romantic novelist, was raised up fifty years after his death as the idol — or, rather, as the pet — of an anti-romantic school of criticism. Meanwhile, the great body of novel-readers began to read him again because they found that, unlike the anti-romantics themselves, he was genial, vigorous, readable, and, within the area included by his blinkers, persuasive.

Thus what has been called his veracity recommended him at the same time, but for different reasons, to the sects and to the general public. Whether it will give immortality to his stories is extremely doubtful. They have none of that intensity which, in a work of art, pierces the heart and mind of readers remote in time and enables them to re-imagine it in terms of their own lives. Many have had pleasure in the company of Lily Dale; in Trollope's day his readers besought him to let her marry Johnny Eames in the end; but has anyone, because of her, rediscovered his own love, or, for the sake of any novel of Trollope's, re-interpreted his own life? If the answer is 'no', it may go hard with Trollope's stories as the generations pass. Veracity between blinkers and an absence of spuriousness, though they are qualities which link him with Miss Austen, are rarely enough to keep novels in print.

Nevertheless the same veracity, applied not to fiction but to fact, may well continue to safeguard the life of the *Autobiography*. The further it recedes in time, the more remarkable it seems to become. There is a pressure within it that is not to be felt in the novels, and it is by no means improbable that a young man today or a hundred or two hundred years hence may lay it down, and stare, and re-imagine his own experience in the light of it. Trollope's plainness was exceedingly odd; he was both pugnacious and accepting. That these seeming contradictions are not mutually exclusive — indeed that no human quality is exclusive of any other — is one of the truths that each opinionated generation has to learn afresh, and the lesson has never been more straightforwardly taught than in Trollope's *Autobiography*.

# LIBER AMORIS

## I

HAZLITT's *Liber Amoris or The New Pygmalion* was published in May, 1823. It was anonymous, but wore a disguise so thin as to deceive no one. It was an account of Hazlitt's frustrated passion for a girl, Sarah, the second daughter of a tailor named Walker, in whose house in London Hazlitt lodged.

The first of the book's three parts was made up of a group of dialogues between the girl and the author; the second was a series of letters, describing the writer's agony and devotion, addressed to 'C.P. Esq', easily identifiable, and P. G. Patmore, father of the poet; and the third consisted of letters to another friend, now known to have been the dramatist, Sheridan Knowles, giving the *dénouement* of the unhappy tale. The manuscript of the book and the originals of the letters to Patmore from which Hazlitt made selection were preserved. In 1894, the whole material was gathered together and privately printed in a volume introduced by Richard Le Gallienne.

Since then P. P. Howe's authoritative *Life* has greatly added to our knowledge of Hazlitt, but Howe's view of his duty was scholarly rather than interpretative, or — to speak more precisely — he preferred to keep himself in the background and to present Hazlitt's life, as far as possible, in the words of those who were witnesses of it. The method had great advantages. It made the biography 'authoritative' in the strictest sense of the word. But it withheld the biographer from any attempt to correct the prejudice by which the *Liber Amoris* has always been surrounded or to re-assess its value.

Such a re-assessment is overdue. In spite of persistent attack, the *Liber Amoris* has stubbornly survived. It was called 'disgusting' by Crabb Robinson, using the word, not in its earlier sense of 'distasteful', but as we use it, violently, to mean 'revolting' or 'repulsive'. Le Gallienne called it 'silly', and, even as late as 1947, so wise and humane a critic as Mr. Frank Swinnerton spoke of it as 'that tragic piece of futility'. And yet it lives with its own life, and not merely because the great essayist wrote it. No one who reads ever forgets it.

One reason is that it constitutes what a lawyer might call a leading case in the psychology of love. It said on the subject something that had not been said before in English prose, and has not been said since with the same directness and candour. What it said, and the value of the evidence it gave, we, in the midst of the twentieth century, are better able to discern than were those Victorians and pre-Victorians to whom its truth was unfamiliar and disturbing. Either they had not read Stendhal or they discounted him as French.

Love has never been, and is not now, an accurate translation of *amour*. Nevertheless ideas, even of love, cross the Channel at last. Stendhal is now familiar to us, and a comparison of the date, 1822, of Stendhal's *De L'Amour*, with that of the *Liber Amoris*, is illuminating. These dates prove beyond doubt that Stendhal wrote independently of Hazlitt, and there is every reason to believe that Hazlitt wrote independently of Stendhal.

2

The 'book of our conversations (I mean mine and the statue's) which I call *Liber Amoris*' was begun at Stamford and dated 29 January 1822. The author was on his way to Edinburgh where, with the assistance of Scottish law more compliant than the English, he and his first wife were to be collusively divorced. In February and March he was at the Renton Inn, Berwickshire (called the Bees Inn in his book), writing 'ten pages a day, which mounts up to thirty guineas worth a week', of those essays, including *Patronage and Puffing* and *On the Fear of Death*, which were to be the second volume of *Table Talk*. At the end of March he went to Edinburgh. Held by the law's delays, beset by agonized hopes and doubts concerning Miss Walker, writing to her and receiving replies (when he received any at all) as non-committal as only a statue's or a cautious servant-girl's could be, writing to Patmore, lecturing, walking in the Highlands with Sheridan Knowles, fencing with his wife who, he feared, might not go through with the divorce after all, Hazlitt loitered in Scotland.

In the latter half of May, he was in London, a lodger again in Southampton Buildings, distracted by Sarah's coldness, even more by her inarticulateness. 'She turned her head and shrunk from my embraces, as if quite alienated or mortally offended. . . . I could get only short, sullen, disconnected answers, as if there were something labouring in her mind which she either could not or would not impart.' This astonished him in the girl who for so many months, when he had formerly lodged under her parents' roof, had spent hours of every day in his room and had permitted and delighted in every intimacy except that last which, because

he idealized her and wished to become her husband, he had
not pressed upon her. He did not understand it. 'I asked
what could it mean?' — and Sarah Walker did not enlighten
him, partly because she had other fish to fry, partly also, we
may hazard, because she was bewildered by a passion she
did not share and, in face of Hazlitt's appalling eloquence
and intensity, fell back upon the little, stiff conventions,
half-pert, half-formal, of her class when ill at ease. Hazlitt
was baffled, furious and enchanted. Aware of his humiliation but accepting it, he begged crumbs of reassurance even
from the girl's mother, who was clearly a bawd. 'I took her
wrinkled, withered, cadaverous, clammy hand at parting and
kissed it. Faugh!'

This stage of the struggle endured nearly a fortnight.
Hazlitt then returned to Scotland where, on 17 July, the
divorce proceedings ended. He was now free to offer marriage to Miss Walker. Meanwhile he had taken soundings.
Was it worth his while to make a formal offer? The girl's
brother-in-law could give no better answer than that he
thought Hazlitt might try his fortune. This he promptly did
'with joy, with something like confidence', and with what
consequences of disillusionment the end of the *Liber Amoris*
tells us.

For a period which began long before Hazlitt's going to
Scotland, she had been playing with another lodger, Mr. C.,
the same game that she had played with him. Now Mr. C.
lived no longer in the house but at a little distance, and
Hazlitt came upon the two walking together. His description
of the encounter has the straightness of Defoe, and at the
end a touch — the recording that they passed *twice* — so
brilliant, so unlikely and so persuasive, so unemphatic and
yet so strikingly true, that it takes the breath away: 'I passed

a house in King-street where I had once lived, and had not proceeded many paces, ruminating on chance and change and old times, when I saw her coming towards me. I felt a strange pang at the sight, but I thought her alone. Some people before me moved on, and I saw another person with her. It was a tall, rather well-looking young man, but I did not at first recollect him. We passed at the crossing of the street without speaking. . . . She went by me without even changing countenance, without expressing the slightest emotion. . . . I turned and looked — they also turned and looked — and as if by mutual consent, we both retrod our steps and passed again, in the same way. I went home.' What do men mean who say that a book which contains such passages as this is 'silly'? The firmness, speed and veracity of it send us all to school.

Worse was to come. Hazlitt and Mr. C. afterwards compared notes. Miss Walker's duplicity was clear. It was not that she had favoured each in turn, but that she had systematically and simultaneously deceived both, while maintaining, as an excuse for keeping Hazlitt in agony, the fiction — was it a fiction? — of a lost adorer to whom her very soul was devoted. Hazlitt abandoned hope, was deluded no more — was deluded no more, that is to say, by Miss Walker herself. 'If there had been the frailty of passion, it would have been excusable; but it is evident she is a practised, callous jilt.' And again: 'Her unmoved indifference and self-possession all the while, show that it is her constant practice. Her look even, if closely examined, bears this interpretation. It is that of studied hypocrisy or startled guilt, rather than of refined sensibility or conscious innocence.' Disillusionment could go no further. 'Were she even to return to her former pretended fondness and endearments, I could have no pleasure, no confidence in them.' And yet, though the girl was nothing, the ideal love, which had (to use Stendhal's word) been crystallized in her, lived on. 'She is dead to me,' Hazlitt wrote in his conclusion, 'but what she once was to me, can never die!'

The whole story of the *Liber Amoris* is a flawless example of Stendhal's theory of crystallization, the more valuable because it was almost certainly written without knowledge of that theory. In 1824, probably in April, Hazlitt married again and on 1 September set out upon a journey through France and Italy. In Paris he met Stendhal for the first time and, Howe tells us, 'Stendhal's *De L'Amour* formed Hazlitt's travelling companion during his tour, and was brought by this means to the knowledge of readers of the *Morning Chronicle*.' It is, of course, not impossible that he had received an earlier copy of the book, but 1824 looks like the date of his first reading it. With thoughts of Miss Walker in his mind, he must have read it with deep attention, for he himself, in the heat of blood, had set down his experience, asking again and again: 'What does it mean? Why am I, who see so clearly, yet so bewitched?' and here was Stendhal telling him precisely why.

Almost too precisely. *De L'Amour* was brilliant analysis. It isolated, and held up for intellectual observation, a truth about love which, though others had expressed it often enough — Shakespeare in his *Sonnets*, for example, and Montaigne in his *Essays* — had never been so isolated before. We know more of ourselves (when we have leisure to examine ourselves) because Stendhal wrote, but we have not, in time of trouble, the mental detachment and coolness necessary to be his pupils. Hazlitt's book, without so well understanding what it says, says the same thing in such a way that passionate youth, or passionate middle-age for that matter, may see, reflected in its pages, an aspect of love which the aloof world calls 'disgusting' or 'silly' or 'futile' and which the passion-stricken one half-knows to be so in himself. Yet he may find, in these same pages, that assuagement which is given by imagination shared, and is, to the tormented and enraptured, more precious than counsel.

### 3

What is this truth that Montaigne knew, and Stendhal reiterated, and Hazlitt exemplified? That we project our own imagining of Love on to her whom we say we love. We re-create her in an ideal shape — Hazlitt called Miss Walker 'the statue' — and worship her in that shape, and struggle to bring the statue to life. 'Like the passion of Love,' said Montaigne, 'that lends Beauties and Graces to the person it does embrace; and that makes those who are caught with it, with a depraved and corrupt Judgment, consider the thing they love other and more perfect than it is.' *

Hazlitt goes further than this, further than Montaigne, further even than Stendhal, in his laying bare of the process of crystallization. He shows, because he is a supreme realist and is unafraid to give himself away, that the crystallizing lover is by no means the blind fool that he is traditionally supposed to be. He thus deprives himself of the only romantic defence with which an aloof and self-righteous world might be disposed contemptuously to cover him. The lover, Hazlitt says in effect, is not even a dupe; he is worse,

* I am indebted for this reference to Montaigne, II, 17 (Cotton's translation) to P. and C. N. S. Woolf's translation of *De L'Amour* (London: Duckworth, 1915).

he is a half-dupe, and yet persists; his desire is, as Shakespeare has said, '*past reason* hunted. . . .'

> 'All this the world well knows, yet none knows well
> To shun the heaven that leads men to this hell.'

Hazlitt made no attempt to dignify his obsession. His division of mind between knowledge of Miss Walker's inadequacy and passionate exaltation of the ideal she represented is made plain in his terrible alternation of blame and praise, of angry distrust and wild confidence, of sickening triviality and high romance. In the *Liber Amoris* as it was published, there is evidence enough of this; in the original letters even more. He urged Patmore to employ a friend, E., to seduce the girl if he could in order that his, Hazlitt's, doubts might be quenched. 'Get someone to try her,' he wrote on 4 July, 'or I am destroyed for ever. To go & see E., then after he [*words obliterated*] her for the asking, would lift my soul from Hell. It would be sweet and full revenge. *You* may try her, if you like. . . . Life is hideous to me, & death horrible. Oh! that I knew she was a strumpet, & that she knew I did.' And four days later, having received news from Patmore which he took to be reassuring, this: 'She is an angel from heaven. . . . She is a saint, an angel, a love. I now worship her, & fall down on my knees in thankfulness to God and Nature for this reprieve at least. . . . I have been thinking of her little face these last two days, looking like a marble statue, as cold, as fixed and graceful as ever statue did, & I could not believe the lies I told of her.'

It is not, to use *Blackwood's* word, 'manly'. The letters, even as they were published, expose their writer to all the shafts of ridicule and contempt. But they are an invaluable document because they are not dressed-up, because they are fearless of being laughed at, because they pour out the vast and the petty inconsistencies of the truth. If they are read contemptuously or in moral indignation, they will yield nothing. If they are read pitifully, they will yield not much more. But if they are read compassionately, in a spirit of 'feeling with', they respond with compassion. That is why no lover who opens the *Liber Amoris* puts it down easily, and why no one who reads — though he resist and hate — ever forgets it.

4

It is an extreme book. For that reason, and because its extremism is sexual, and because it was written by genius and, therefore, not palely but with blood, it has hitherto been a cause either of rage or of bridling and embarrassment in many readers. Even today, after the lapse of a century and a quarter, it will not be received dispassionately; nor should it be; it is not a dispassionate book: you pick up what might, after so many years, be a spent ember, and it burns.

Nevertheless, we may hope, as our predecessors could not, to see the *Liber Amoris* as it is in itself and to judge it by its faults and virtues in its own kind. Our intolerances, even when political, are not those of Hazlitt's age, and, even when sexual, are no longer of the sort that made Crabb Robinson cry out, after reading the book, that 'it ought to exclude the author from all decent society'.

The reasons for its having been attacked with so much vehemence are plain. They were at first political; then, in the Victorian age, conventionally moral.

Hazlitt was an independent. Neither in life nor in literature did he run for shelter into any school, and he had no organized claque to support him. His opinions, tenaciously maintained, conformed to no system recognized by his contemporaries. Though conservative by temperament, a lover of the past, a profound loyalist to the memories of his childhood and youth, he was an unswerving hater of the Bourbons. An admirer of Burke's *Reflections*, he yet regarded himself as a child of the French Revolution. An apostle of Freedom in the abstract, he adored Napoleon. 'I am no politician,' he wrote, 'and still less of a party man,' but party men, then as now, were determined to engage artists on one side or the other, and the anti-Jacobins were out for Hazlitt's blood. The appearance of the *Liber Amoris* was a heaven-sent opportunity to his enemies. *Blackwood's* reviewer let himself go. The book, he observed with delight, was 'not a creation of mere Cockney imagination, but a *veritable* transcript of the feelings and doings of an individual living LIBERAL'. He then quoted the passages which seemed to him the most damagingly licentious, identified the publisher, John Hunt, as the publisher of the *Liberal* and the *Examiner* and as the brother of Leigh Hunt, and, with a triumphant flourish, left the examples quoted — as final damnation of the Cockney School — 'in the hands of every single individual, however humble in station, however limited in knowledge or acquirement, who has elevation enough to form the least notion of what "virtue", "honour" and "manliness", and, we may add, "love" mean — and penetration enough to understand a plain English story told in plain English.'

This is fustian, but there is no denying that, *Blackwood's* being then what *Blackwood's* was, Hazlitt had asked for it. The *Liber Amoris* is a vulnerable book. Nothing is easier than to quote from it derisively. Even to the point of self-humiliation in the little shames Hazlitt, following Rousseau, had not hesitated to give himself away, and the reviewer did only what was to be expected of him. There is, moreover, a sense in which it is true to say that the *Liber Amoris* is a failure. It is not, even within its own intention, the great book it might have been; it does not take rank — and no one can have been more bitterly aware of this than its author — with or near the *Confessions* of Rousseau or *La Nouvelle Héloïse*. It was written too close in time to the experience from which it sprang. The period of distillation was too short, and its shortness prevented Hazlitt from entering imaginatively into Sarah Walker's mind.

## 5

It was a mind which presents interesting problems to an imaginative reader of Hazlitt's book, above all to a novelist; and it is worth while to turn aside for a moment to examine what evidence there is about Sarah Walker. What was her own point of view? Why did she behave as she did, and what account of her behaviour did she give to herself?

Her appearance is relevant, and of this we have some knowledge. She had a rare grace of movement, an air of gliding or wafting herself across a room without visibly taking steps. Procter, quoted by Birrell, speaks of her snake-like walk, and Hazlitt, evidently thinking of her when he wrote his essay *On Living to One's Self*, quoted Procter's Mirandola:

> With what a waving air she goes
> Along the corridor. How like a fawn!
> Yet statelier! Hark! No sound, however soft,
> Nor gentlest echo telleth where she treads,
> But every motion of her shape doth seem
> Hallowed by silence —

and we receive an impression continually of a girl whose bodily movement had in it a quality of reticence, beautiful but mysterious, as though she were trying to make herself invisible.

Her face seems not to have been beautiful by any standard ordinarily accepted then or now. It was small and round — so far, perhaps, so good; but the eyes were bad. 'Glassy', says an independent witness, and Hazlitt, having spoken of them as 'timidly cast upon the ground', makes us feel that they were exceedingly uncomfortable when they looked up. There was then, he said in his *Table Talk*, 'a cold, sullen, watery, glazed look about the eyes, which she bent upon vacancy, as if determined to avoid all explanation with yours'. The charitable may say that the girl needed spectacles, but there seems to have been more in it than that. 'Glassy' and 'glazed' are not pleasant words. Hazlitt speaks also of 'their glittering, motionless surface'. Such eyes accord too well with the snake-like movement.

And yet she was 'demure, pretty, modest-looking', and, above all, gave Hazlitt the impression that she genuinely loved him. This, to him, was of supreme importance. He was a suspicious, shy man who, though his intimate friends, such as Lamb, were fond of him, did not make easy first impressions and believed himself to be disliked. In his youth, Crabb Robinson tells us, Hazlitt 'was excessively shy, and in company the girls always made game of him. He had a horror of the society of ladies, especially of smart and handsome and modest young women.' Add to this that he was of sensual temperament, deeply serious and conscious of his own powers. The desire not to be 'teased' by pretty girls, as Crabb Robinson's friend Miss Kitchener teased him, is comprehensible.

Sarah Walker was not 'smart' or, in the formidably social sense of the word, 'handsome'. It was at any rate not by chatter that she teased him. She was accessible to caresses, she spent hours with him willingly; she did not madden him with that clamorous frivolity of which Miss Kitchener may be suspected. On the contrary she was silent by habit. While sitting on his knee and embracing him, she listened — as though it were the words she enjoyed — to the talk of the man who could hold the audience at Lamb's; she kissed him and yet was demure; he quoted and she let him quote; he worshipped and she let him worship. She was neither so chaste as to freeze, nor so unchaste as to alarm, him. Her passivity and listlessness prevented her from giggling genius down. It was easy for him to believe that she, alone among women, appreciated and loved him.

The simple and probably inadequate explanation of Miss Walker is that she was an early nineteenth-century equivalent of what is nowadays called a 'good-timer' — a girl, that is to say, with no rule except her own pleasure but without the capacity or courage to drink pleasure deep; a weak creature seeking always the petty re-assurances of vanity; anaemically indifferent rather than callous; desiring change not for adventure's sake but to cheat the natural emptiness of her mind; conventional, defensive, always afraid of missing something, an intuitive hater of distinction, vulgarly refined. Miss Walker had some of these qualities, but the character does not fit her. It does not fit her because it is a mass-product, and she, whatever her faults, was not mass-produced.

It seems by no means improbable that, before she met Hazlitt, she had loved in her fashion a man who had vanished from her life. She said so; she gave it as her reason for holding

Hazlitt back; and the man is more likely to have existed than to have been invented by her. That he was altogether a fiction, it is hard to believe, and, if he existed, she may well have crystallized in him her idea of love, and so have become, as it were, chilled against all but the minor sensualities in which she indulged with Hazlitt and Mr. C. All that we are told of her suggests that she was in some sense numb rather than naturally cold or deliberately cruel.

Haydon says that the dialogues given in the *Liber Amoris* were 'literal'. They bear the stamp of truth. Consider, then, these passages:

H.  Tell me why you have deceived me, and singled me out as your victim?
S.  I never have, Sir. I always said I could not love. . . . I have always been consistent from the first.

Hazlitt demands why, then, she had kissed him at first asking. She had seemed 'so reserved and modest' that 'whatever favours you granted must proceed from pure regard'. To a long tirade, she answers only: 'I am no prude, Sir'. Then, later:

S.  I'll stay and hear this no longer.
H.  Yes, one word more. Did you not love another?
S.  Yes, and ever shall most sincerely.

Hazlitt himself believed it at the time, for he replied: 'Then *that* is my only hope'. Sarah never swerved from it.

Hazlitt came afterwards to believe that she had lied. It was an explanation supplied by rage and disappointment. If he had waited until he was able to recollect his emotion in tranquillity and had then re-imagined Miss Walker, he might have seen himself as she, perhaps, saw him: a man different from any she had formerly known, belonging to a world she had never guessed at, having powers she had never felt. His imagination, the force of crystallization that drove him mad, could not be without its effect on her. She was, or thought of herself as being, ordinary; but imagination has creative power, and this extraordinary man was imagining her as an extraordinary girl. She was on her own ground with Mr. C. across the passage; he passed the time; but what was she to do with Mr. Hazlitt? Not love him — as well love a whirl-wind. Not marry him — as well marry a creature from Mars. And not abruptly repel him for many reasons — mixed reasons, good and bad: that he was a profitable lodger and she her mother's daughter; that she had, in any case, to wait on him and life had to be lived; that she was more than a little in awe of him; and, to do her credit, that he was often kind, and gave her presents, and she did not wish to offend him. Moreover, she was, in some obscure way, grateful to him — not, as he once implied, for the present only, but be-cause he made her feel important. She could not explain; she had not the language; she had not even the consecutive thought in which to explain herself to herself. What, then, should she do? She could, if he liked it, put her arms round him, and kiss him, and, being an animal, like it too. Perhaps she was deceiving him, for Mr. C. belonged to a different compartment of her mind.

Whether, if he had given himself time, Hazlitt would have interpreted her in this way or another, he would certainly, being an artist, have interpreted her from the inside. That he did not do so unbalances his book if we consider it as we might consider a novel. From that point of view, it is in-complete. But this very one-sidedness, this extreme subjec-tivity, gives it rare value as a document written at white-heat by a man of genius at the height of passionate obsession. At the time Hazlitt was afflicted by the terrible loquaciousness which is often a consequence of spiritual loneliness and despair. Being a man, he did what many a man before him has done in his condition: he went from friend to friend, from acquaintance to acquaintance, boring them all, telling his story — to him a tragedy, to them almost a farce — again and again. Finding Haydon from home, he poured it all out to Haydon's manservant, Sammons; then, on the same day, going to inspect lodgings in Pimlico and meeting a landlady who said he did not look well — 'the devil take me, if I did not let out the whole story from beginning to end!'

So the man, suffering to the point of insanity. But Hazlitt was also a writer. The *Liber Amoris* was his relief. It has the defect of being unbalanced in its treatment of, or in its failure to treat with interior sympathy, the other protagonist of the tale. But balance, except in very dull leading articles and very pedestrian men, is not all. Pressure is one of the evidences of genius, and another, when you can write Hazlitt's prose, is a complete carelessness for the moderate and unsentimental sneer that will greet the end of your sentence. Hazlitt wrote this: '. . . I am now inclosed in a dungeon of despair. The sky is marble to my thoughts; nature is dead around me, as hope is within me; no object can give me one gleam of satisfaction now, nor the prospect of it in time to come. I wander by the sea-side; and the eternal ocean and lasting despair and her face are before me. Slighted by her, on whom my heart by its last fibre hung, where shall I turn? I wake with her by my side, not as my sweet bed-fellow, but as the corpse of my love, without a heart in her bosom, cold, insensible, or struggling from me; and the worm gnaws me, and the sting of unrequited love, and the canker of a hopeless, endless sorrow. I have lost the taste of my food by feverish anxiety; and my favourite beverage, which used to refresh me when I got up, has no moisture in it. Oh! cold, solitary, sepulchral breakfast. . . .' Who will may smile at that. It is extreme, unbalanced, and, fortunately, without a sense of humour. But it is true with a truth that a regulated and discreet sanity could not have communicated. 'The sky is marble to my thoughts,' wrote Hazlitt, and the saying is of Shakespeare's breed. It has the terrible flash of *Troilus and Cressida*.

But it was neither Hazlitt's failure to re-imagine Miss Walker nor his 'sepulchral breakfasts' that provoked *Blackwood's* rage. The reviewer condemned the book for its principal merit — its treatment of love. He may say what he pleases about 'virtue', 'honour' and 'manliness'. They are words used by him to create fashionable prejudice, and, at this distance of time, are not worth disputing, but to say that Hazlitt did not know the meaning of love, and to say no more than this, was to beg the whole question that the *Liber Amoris* presents for judgement.

6

Whether *Blackwood's* reviewer was as shocked as he pretended to be we may a little doubt; he was, presumably, a child of the eighteenth century; but that the Victorians were genuinely shocked is certain and understandable. Stevenson abandoned a project of writing Hazlitt's Life because Hazlitt had written the *Liber Amoris*, and when, at the end of the century, Augustine Birrell wrote on Hazlitt in the English Men of Letters Series, he approached Miss Walker with contortions of reluctance and held out the *Liber Amoris* with a pair of tongs. 'The loves of the middle-aged,' he began, forgetful of Antony, 'are never agreeable subject-matter for the pens of third parties. "A fool at forty is a fool indeed", and

M

this affair of Hazlitt's must be briefly handled.' He then rehearsed the facts which were, he said, by now 'offensively
familiar', and concluded: 'Anyhow, the whole sentimental
structure of the *Liber Amoris* now sinks below the stage, and
joins the realm of things unspeakable — "vile kitchen
stuff", fit only for the midden.'

This is fierce prejudice; if we can understand it, we may
the better understand the book which provoked it, for the
value of the *Liber Amoris* is that it expresses a kind of love
— no less love for being also a kind of madness — which a
great part of Victorian opinion persisted in regarding as in-
human baseness, so vile and so exceptional that it was not a
fit subject for literature or even for thought. From this point
of view, passion — of which the existence could scarcely be
denied by readers of *Romeo and Juliet* — was seen as a
lamentable intrusion upon the ordered decencies of society.
It was, therefore, carefully distinguished, as an aberration,
from that love which conformed to the social rule. When it
appeared in the very young, it was treated, unless it led to
extra-matrimonial disaster, as a naïveté to be wryly smiled
at, and, if it could not be suppressed, to be tolerated under
the name of calf-love. In all other circumstances, it was ruth-
lessly hunted, as it was in Parnell; and, in order that it might
be hunted, it had first to be outlawed — that is to say, it had
to be proclaimed as something freakish and unnatural, abnormal as crime is abnormal. This attitude towards passion,
and a corresponding attitude towards crystallization, were
expressed by Richard Le Gallienne (1894) with the ingenuous candour of the period. 'Though, as we have seen, the
illusion did credit to Hazlitt's heart, it is impossible not to
feel that no man of forty should be able to mistake a woman
for a goddess or an angel. . . . It is unnatural, uncanny, in

the bearded man. Naïveté is charming up to twenty, but the naïveté of middle-age is unattractive, and the *Liber Amoris* is full of that unattractive quality, — much like the naïveté we sometimes find in the poetical effusions of criminals.'

It is an adroit piece of special pleading. To mistake a woman for a goddess would indeed be naïve, but this precisely is what Hazlitt did not do. He saw the woman and the goddess at the same time; was agonizingly aware both of the distinction between them on one plane of his consciousness and of their identity on another plane; was unceasingly observant of his self-division; was the sane, unsparing analyst of his own madness, and, therefore, racked.

## 7

That this was possible and in the nature of passion, the upholders of Victorian convention would not admit. They would not admit it because to have done so would have been to let in a flood which must destroy, and has since destroyed, their world. They were not, as their detractors are at last beginning to understand, blind. Still less were they complacent. They saw what was coming. As the century drew towards its end, they fought, in fear for their society, a long defensive battle for the values upon which it was based. It was as clear to them as it is to us that sexual passion is a dominant force which in a stable society must be harnessed. Their method of harnessing it was to equate love with respect, respect with reason, reason with constancy; and to discountenance all love, and all books about love (except Shakespeare's), which did not conform to this theory.

Two things necessarily followed of which the rigidity, often unjustly called the hypocrisy, of their matrimonial code was only an outward manifestation: first, the outlawing of passion felt to be subversive; second, a refusal to recognize that it is possible and even natural to respect and not respect at the same time, to despise and worship, to be mean and generous, cruel and kind, a sensual slave and a true lover, not only in turns but *at the same time*. The wiser among them were not ignorant of this; they had read their Shakespeare and had lived their own lives; but they would not give their knowledge recognition because they feared that to give social effect to the tendency of the human personality to fragment would be to disintegrate society itself. That they were unjustified in their fear, we, in whom they would see the justification of it, dare not assert. We examine the fragments of the human personality as they did not, but the twentieth century has found no alternative to their admittedly artificial integration.

This is not to say that no alternative exists. If it can be found, and when it can be found, the breakdown of the Victorian artifice may be counted as a gain. We are at any rate to this extent liberated: that we no longer fear to read Shakespeare in the context of our own lives.

> My love is as a fever, longing still
> For that which longer nurseth the disease;
> Feeding on that which doth preserve the ill,
> The uncertain sickly appetite to please.
> My reason, the physician to my love,
> Angry that his prescriptions are not kept,
> Hath left me, and I desperate now approve
> Desire is death, which physic did except.
> Past cure I am, now reason is past care,
> And frantic-mad with evermore unrest;
> My thoughts and my discourse as madmen's are,
> At random from the truth vainly express'd;
>   For I have sworn thee fair, and thought thee bright,
>   Who art as black as hell, as dark as night.

It is a sonnet that might have stood as epigraph to the *Liber Amoris*, which also tells a little of what suffering humanity has to learn of its own unreason.

> Who taught thee how to make me love thee more,
> The more I hear and see just cause of hate?

It is Shakespeare's question and Hazlitt's too. Is it criminal naïveté? Is it, even, a rare question? Happy the man or woman who never has cause to ask it! Happy — or dead. Happy as the Brownings were — or dead as they were not.

# TURGENEV'S *FIRST LOVE* *
### or
## TURGENEV'S TREATMENT OF A LOVE-STORY

IT is remarkable that, throughout the Western world, there
is today a renewed interest in Turgenev, for, in more ways
than one, Turgenev is a 'test case'. Our judgement of him
must govern many other of our judgements in literature and
in life. To recognize him as a great master is to profess our
adherence to certain values which, taken together, almost
define civilization itself; to shrug our shoulders at him, to
think of him as a romantic aesthete whose work is no longer
relevant to us, is, in effect, to renounce Western civilization
as an inheritance from Greece and from Christianity, and to
adopt an altogether different view of the nature of man and
of his place in the scheme of things.

There are few writers of whom this is equally true, or true
with the same intensity, as it is of Turgenev. It is equally
true of Keats; to reject him is to reject what I mean by
civilization; but it is not equally true of other novelists of
Turgenev's rank — of Tolstoy, for example, or of Dickens
— who, though not themselves materialists, sometimes used
the polemical method of the materialists. I mean that they,
even in their art, could be didactic and aggressive as Turgenev was not. They were prepared, on occasion, to shout
and scold, to regiment, to condemn, to exclude, but he,

* The Giff Edmonds Memorial Lecture. Delivered before the Royal
Society of Literature, London, 1947.

though he could be irritable as a man, was, as an artist, tolerant, compassionate and forgiving unto seventy times seven. It follows that collective materialists, though they cannot approve of Tolstoy's Christianity or of Dickens's evident warmth of heart, can approve of their angers as they cannot approve of that persistent gentleness in Turgenev which they call his indifference.

With his care for beauty of expression, his everlasting quest of formal perfection, his interest in men and women as such rather than in the classes into which they happen to be divided, he seemed to many in his own day, and has seemed to many since, too accepting, too aloof. Those revolutionaries in Russia, whose ideals he partly shared but whose illusions he smiled at, felt intuitively, and rightly, that, in his view, the violent substitution of one tyranny for another would be no great gain. They considered it apostasy in him that he should spend so great a part of his life in France, writing love stories, when he might have been at their grindstone, grinding their axe.

Their successors have adopted and sharpened the contemporary objections to Turgenev: his forbearance, his patience, his refusal to believe in the perfectibility of society under any system; above all, the concentration of his genius, not on systems or on classes or even on men's collective fate, but on that infinite variety of human relationship in which, for him, the spirit of man was articulated. It is this that makes of Turgenev, as it does not of Tolstoy, so clear a dividing line between two opposed readings of life: the reading of the Western world, and of the great religions of the East, which rests ultimately upon the value of each man and each woman as a creature, and the materialistic reading which, when carried to an extreme, treats men and women

as animals who have no power to transcend their environment, who have no spiritual life independent of it, and who,
therefore, in the utmost confusion of mind, are to regard
themselves as being, in some sort, creatures of the State
which they themselves created.

In the view of those who read life in these terms, art is not,
and cannot be, a spiritual act. To treat it as such is, they say,
to be a pretender. Again, in their view, love is not, and cannot be, anything else than a biological act. To treat it otherwise is to be romantic. The real difference between Turgenev
and his materialistic critics is not of wealth or of power, but
of fundamental values, and it is a difference which nowadays
divides the world. His reality was for them delusion; what
he considered delusion was, and still is, their reality.

2

This might be illustrated throughout the whole range of
his works, and particularly in his treatment of those characters which are directly or indirectly political. It used to be a
habit of those who admired Turgenev to defend him vigor-
ously against a charge of what was then called 'escapism'.
They would point to Bazarov in *Fathers and Children* as
being unquestionably a political character, and would discover sociological symbols even in his portraits of women,
saying that they represented the New Woman or the New
Russia or what you will. Even that wise man Edward Gar-
nett thought it worth while to attempt to placate Turgenev's
opponents in this way, and a recent biographer, Mr. Lloyd,
has urged us to remember that Turgenev 'depicted the
Nihilist who was to flower eventually in the cold logic of
Lenin'.

Such an approach to Turgenev is not unreasonable, but

as the years pass it seems more and more to lay emphasis in the wrong place. It is true that Turgenev disliked serfdom, censorship and bureaucracy; the Tsar said that his early writings had contributed to the abolition of serfdom in 1861. It is true that he was a liberal thinker and that all his works, from *A Sportsman's Sketches* onward, were on the side of political freedom wherever it happened, in the natural course of his narrative, to become an issue. But he did not make it a principal issue, and his studies of serfdom are altogether different from those that would have been written by a man for whom emancipation was an end in itself or by one who was fully convinced that good — the good he cared for — would be a consequence of this, or indeed of any other, political act. What emerges from his studies of peasants is not an imperative longing for a shift of political power, certainly not an incitement to rebellion, but an intense personal insight into this man or this woman. It was for this reason that he gave equal offence to the stupider landowners on the Right and to the more arid politicians on the Left. Both, from their opposite points of view, saw the peasants as a herd. He did not. Looking at a peasant, who was outwardly almost a dumb animal, he was not — how shall it be said? — he was not *exteriorized* by that dumbness. He entered imaginatively into the peasant's life, into the peasant's own sense of identity, and looked out upon the world with his or her eyes. Looking out, he encountered his own eyes looking in. The result, in one after another of the sketches and above all in his story of the peasant Mumu who was deaf and dumb, was a sympathy — a 'feeling with' that is nobler than pity, a communication and fusing of individual spirit with individual spirit, that was unique, and was at once felt to be unique, in Russian literature.

But this power did not make political pamphlets of *A Sportsman's Sketches* or of any of Turgenev's works. His opponents are, in this matter, unquestionably right. Though of a liberal mind, he was not an immediately effective politician, and we who love him do wrong to pretend that he was, or even that politics, which implies thinking of men in groups and in terms of group-action, was among his principal interests. We must not play into the hands of his opponents by weakly attempting to appease them. Turgenev was primarily an artist; do not let us pretend that he was primarily a politician or a sociologist. We do no service to any man's memory, and certainly none to the cause of good criticism and clear thinking, if, in order to recommend him to materialists, we pretend that he was what he was not.

Turgenev was of an aristocratic, not of a vulgar or, even, a popular mind. He was of a romantic, aesthetic and highly individualistic temperament. He was not a successful pamphleteer or even, at heart, an ardent reformer. He was much more interested in the strange variability of the human, and particularly the feminine, intelligence and passion than he was in any collective plan for our improvement.

I am sure that there are some who will, therefore, frown upon him and think that I am playing my cards very badly when I recommend him to a modern audience in these terms. They are entitled to frown; their brows, high or low, are their own to do with what they will; but they must not expect us yet, in this country, to fall into the totalitarian habit of praising artists for the wrong reasons. Therefore I repeat that though, by the standards of his time, Turgenev was presumably pink, I do not put that forward as a sop to Russophils. Indeed, I regard it as irrelevant. It is of much more interest to observe uncompromisingly that he was indeed aristocratic, romantic, aesthetic, highly individualistic, and that, in spite of this or because of it, his works, after a long period of neglect, are, in England, in France and in America, being everywhere retranslated, republished and newly discussed.

That is why I said at the outset that Turgenev was a 'test case', and why I believe that his treatment of love — that is to say, of human nature, as he saw it, in its loveliest, its most tragic, its most fateful, and always its most revealing imaginative essence — is the key to the whole matter: the evidence upon which his case (and, by implication, the test case of civilization itself) is to be decided.

Let me, in order to be plain, state the issue in crude simplicity. If, when you see a woman, whether she be peasant or lady, what you are interested in is her uniqueness and the mystery of creation implied in that uniqueness; if the impulse of your mind is not to obliterate her uniqueness in a group or a category, but to emphasize it by entering into her being and re-imagining it from the inside outwards; if she is, for you, in her virtues and sins, her wisdom and follies, a private and a holy thing, and holy because private; if in her age you can read her childhood, in her gaiety her seriousness, in her sin her innocence, in her failure her aspiration, and even in her stupidities her dreams; if, in her flesh, her spirit appears; if, therefore, her love is, for you, an image, held for however brief an instant in however dark a mirror, of her immortality, and not simply a part of her animalism; if love is an emblem of wonder, of breed, of distinctiveness, and not a dull mechanism of repetitive fecundity; if to that extent and in that way you are in charity with your neighbour, then you are a romantic, you are a Turgenevian. But if, when you see a woman, whether she be peasant or lady, she is for you primarily a numbered inmate of the economic concentration camp and her love a compulsion to replenish it with slaves, then you are not a Turgenevian. This is the issue, and this is why an examination of Turgenev's treatment of love is, I think, of more than academic interest. It was for him, as it was for Keats, a key to life. We have to decide whether the key is truly made, whether it turns in the lock, and whether, when the door opens — if it does open — a real world or, as Turgenev's detractors say, a falsely romantic world, is revealed. It may also be of interest to look over the locksmith's shoulder and observe his craftsmanship.

### 3

This examination might be made in various ways. The method which I hope you will allow me to adopt is to choose one masterpiece and concentrate upon it; to thank heaven that it is short and its anecdote simple — for nothing is more tedious than the re-telling of an elaborate plot; to call in other witnesses as a matter of convenience now and then; but to invite you to consider Turgenev's method chiefly in the light of this one story.

It may be justly objected that, in other stories, altogether different characters are concerned in altogether different circumstances, and it is true that, if I were a German Professor and you were a German audience, we should not venture to build our house upon so simple a plan or, as the Germans would say, upon so narrow a foundation. But as we are unregenerate English; and as, I think, the foundation, though small, is pretty deep; and as, after all, this is Wednesday afternoon and the sun is shining, let us take our chance. 'Let us roll all our strength and all Our sweetness up into one ball', and examine the story called *First Love*. There are two good reasons for clinging to it: that it is enchanting; and that it is the only story in the world of which I am prepared to say that it is flawless. And that it is the only story of Turgenev's of which I can hope, as a result of much industry, to pronounce the Russian names without being sent by Mr. Harold Nicolson, who I believe has been taking lessons lately, right down to the bottom of the class.

### 4

The story is told by Vladimir Petrovitch, remembering his youth, and this is how it begins:

> I was sixteen then. It happened in the summer of 1833.
> I lived in Moscow with my parents. They had taken a country house for the summer near the Kalouga gate, facing the Neskuchny gardens. I was preparing for the university, but did not work much and was in no hurry.
> No one interfered with my freedom . . .

You will see at once what I meant when I said that the story was flawless. When we remember how many stories, in order to be impressive or mysterious, in order, perhaps, to avert a charge of being old-fashioned, begin with elaborately confused dialogue between persons unknown, in a place unknown, at a time unknown, and leave us to fog it all out halfway through the second chapter, what a relief it is to observe the simplicity of the great masters' attack. Listen to a few others:

> On an evening in the latter part of May a middle-aged man was walking homeward from Shaston to the village of Marlott . . .

— that is Hardy.

> The class was busy studying, when the headmaster entered followed by a new scholar. Turning to the master in charge, he

said in a low voice: 'Monsieur Roger, here is a pupil I especially recommend to your care . . .'

— that is Flaubert.

Happy families are all alike; every unhappy family is unhappy in its own way. Everything was in confusion in the Oblonskys' house. The wife had discovered that the husband was carrying on an intrigue with a French girl . . .

— that is Tolstoy, not a supreme formalist as Turgenev was, but just as careful to be plain at the outset, to engage the reader's attention, to inform him quite simply of what is afoot.

Turgenev sometimes allows himself a little prelude in which to introduce a narrator, but his opening of his main story has always the same firmness and lucidity. Here is another opening of his:

It was in the summer of 1840. Sanin was in his twenty-second year, and he was in Frankfurt on his way home from Italy to Russia . . .

— that is the beginning of *The Torrents of Spring*. But, it may be asked, is there only one way to begin a story? No: there are a thousand ways. In every story, according to how much or how little retrospect it carries, according to whether the writer's talent and style give him the greater command of retrospect or of directly advancing narrative, there is a *right* point of attack; and we, who try to tell stories, choose it wrongly at our peril. To choose it rightly is the hardest of all our tasks. To begin too soon or to begin too late is the greatest of all our confusions. But once that choice is rightly made — (and Turgenev's choice was always accurate; he is never to be seen floundering in too much retrospect or starving for lack of it) — then, I believe that there is a rule: namely, to establish, with the greatest possible economy of means, the place, the persons and time, to arouse the reader's attention, and to announce the theme.

Turgenev's theme, in the story we are considering, is a double one: youth itself, the feel of being young and alive; and love. He loses no time in saying so; he never, never commits the sin of confusing a reader, of leaving him to wonder what the story is about and what he, Turgenev, is driving at. Vladimir Petrovitch has a horse to ride:

I used to saddle it myself and set off alone for long rides, break into a rapid gallop and fancy myself a knight in a tournament.

That indicates at once the youthfulness of the young man and the fate that awaits him, for a knight in a tournament presupposes a lady whose favour he wears. Already, because Turgenev chose that brilliantly accurate phrase, we see the gleam of her eyes — but not yet the lady; she is anonymous; she is felt to exist, but her universality is as yet not limited — is not 'crystallized', as Stendhal would have said — in a personality and a name. This is deliberate. In holding his heroine back, Turgenev is doing much more than prepare an entrance for her; he is making it clear that what he is writing about is love itself, and femininity itself, and not only a particular animal passion. So, in his next paragraph, he continues:

I remember that at that time the image of woman, the vision of love, scarcely ever arose in definite shape in my brain; but in all I thought, in all I felt, lay hidden a half-conscious, shamefaced presentiment of something new, unutterably sweet, feminine. . . . This presentiment, this expectation, permeated my whole being; I breathed in it, it coursed through my veins with every drop of blood . . . it was destined to be soon fulfilled.

It was destined to be very soon fulfilled. Turn one page, and you are plunged into the enchantment. Near to the house in which Vladimir Petrovitch and his parents were living that summer was a dilapidated lodge. This had been rented by an impoverished Princess Zasyekin, herself *une femme très vulgaire* but the widow of an aristocrat. The gardens were separated by a fence, and Vladimir Petrovitch was in the habit of wandering about his garden every evening on the look-out for rooks. Now observe Turgenev's magic — how, in a few lines, he communicates, not a photograph of the girl, scarcely even a sketch of her character and appearance, and yet what I can only call the *flash* of her, and how that flash fires the trail in Vladimir Petrovitch, and how the flame leaps and runs within him.

Suddenly I heard a voice; I looked across the fence, and was thunder-struck. . . . I was confronted with a curious spectacle.

A few paces from me on the grass between the green raspberry bushes stood a tall slender girl in a striped pink dress, with a white kerchief on her head; four young men were close round her, and she was slapping them by turns on the forehead with those small grey flowers, the name of which I don't know, though they are well known to children; the flowers form little bags, and burst open with a pop when you strike them against anything hard. The young men presented their foreheads so eagerly, and in the gestures of the girl (I saw her in profile), there was something so fascinating, imperious, caressing, mocking, and charming, that I almost cried out with admiration and delight, and would, I thought, have given everything in the world on the spot only to have had those exquisite fingers strike me on the forehead. My gun slipped on to the grass, I forgot everything, I devoured with my eyes the graceful shape and neck and lovely arms and the slightly disordered fair hair under the white kerchief, and the half-closed clever eye, and the eyelashes and the soft cheek beneath them . . .

'Young man, hey, young man,' said a voice suddenly near me: 'is it quite permissible to stare so at unknown young ladies?'

I started, I was struck dumb. . . . Near me, the other side of the fence, stood a man with close-cropped black hair, looking ironically at me. At the same instant the girl too turned towards me. . . . I caught sight of big grey eyes in a bright mobile face, and the whole face suddenly quivered and laughed, there was a flash of white teeth, a droll lifting of the eye-brows. . . . I crimsoned, picked up my gun from the ground, and pursued by a musical but not ill-natured laugh, fled to my own room, flung myself on the bed, and hid my face in my hands. My heart was fairly leaping; I was greatly ashamed and overjoyed; I felt an excitement I had never known before.

After a rest, I brushed my hair, washed, and went downstairs to tea. The image of the young girl floated before me, my heart was no longer leaping, but was full of a sort of sweet oppression.

'Full of a sort of sweet oppression.' Remember Keats's phrase, describing the impact upon him of such a girl: 'I feel escaped from a new and threatening sorrow. . . . There is an awful warmth about my heart like a load of immortality.' But let Turgenev continue. For a little while the threat of sorrow is concealed by a wonderful lightness of heart.

'What's the matter?' my father asked me all at once: 'have you killed a rook?'
I was on the point of telling him all about it, but I checked myself, and merely smiled to myself. As I was going to bed, I rotated — I don't know why — three times on one leg, pomaded my hair, got into bed, and slept like a top all night. Before morning I woke up for an instant, raised my head, looked round me in ecstasy, and fell asleep again.

On that I will at present offer no comment. I said that the story was flawless. This opening of it is the first, but still not the chief, of my witnesses.

5

Let me now glance here and there at Turgenev's development of his heroine, who is Zinaïda Alexandrovna, the old Princess's daughter. As the tale is told by Vladimir in the

N

first person, we see her always from the outside, and yet what we chiefly see is not her outside, but a glow from within her. Next morning Vladimir Petrovitch is sent with a message to the dilapidated lodge. He is presented to Zinaïda and she carries him off to wind wool. She is twenty-one, he sixteen; she laughs at him a little for being so young and he pretends to be older than he is.

She was sitting with her back to a window covered with a white blind. . . . 'And here I am sitting before her,' I thought; 'I have made acquaintance with her . . . what happiness, my God!' I could hardly keep from jumping up from my chair in ecstasy, but I only swung my legs a little, like a small child who has been given sweetmeats.

Then a young hussar comes and gives Zinaïda a kitten.

'For the kitten — your little hand,' said the hussar, with a simper and a shrug of his strongly built frame, which was tightly buttoned up in a new uniform.
'Both,' replied Zinaïda, and she held out her hands to him. While he was kissing them, she looked at me over his shoulder. I stood stockstill. . . .

It is a small but perfect instance of what I mean when I say — and I am afraid I have said it often — that an artist's duty is not to teach, to persuade, not even to describe, but to impregnate the imagination of a reader; to draw back a curtain and to say: 'Look out, there is Zinaïda; see her with your own eyes! . . . Look out, there is a world to be created; create it yourself!' 'While he was kissing them, she looked at me over his shoulder.' How? With what expression? With what glance? Provocatively? Derisively? Affectionately? Gaily? Sadly? We are not told. Any adverb would have spoiled that effect — would have 'exteriorized' us, would have made us observers of the outside of Zinaïda instead of drawing us into her, and compelling us, if we would see at all, to look out of her eyes, and to see, over the hussar's shoulder but from within her soul, Vladimir Petrovitch standing 'stockstill'. And any adverb would, correspondingly, have narrowed our sense of that glance's effect on Vladimir Petrovitch. Turgenev knows how to leave well alone. Not until the end of the chapter, when the boy has gone home, does he seek an echo.

'Why is it she's always laughing?' I thought, as I went back home escorted by Fyodor, who said nothing to me, but walked behind me with an air of disapprobation. My mother scolded me and wondered whatever I could have been doing so long at the princess's. I made her no reply and went off to my room. I felt suddenly very sad . . . I tried hard not to cry . . . I was jealous of the hussar.

Soon afterwards the old Princess and her daughter dine at the Voldemars', and we receive Turgenev's first clear indication, very subtly conveyed, that what he is writing is not only a sketch of idealistic first-love but a profound tragi-comedy of passion and the slavery of passion. Vladimir Petrovitch's mother, after the manner of mothers on such occasions, does not approve of her visitors, certainly not of Zinaïda.

'A conceited minx,' she said next day. 'And fancy, what she has to be conceited about, avec sa mine de grisette!'
'It's clear you have never seen any grisettes,' my father observed to her.
'Thank God, I haven't!'
'Thank God, to be sure . . . only how can you form an opinion of them, then?'

What is to happen is that Zinaïda, to whom all men are slaves and who cannot resist the pride of tormenting them, is herself to become the slave of Vladimir's father; and this fragment of dialogue is Turgenev's premonitory hint. The cruelty of passion, hitherto a weapon in Zinaïda's hands, is to turn its point back upon her. She whom we first saw slapping her adorers with small grey flowers that burst open with a pop on their foreheads; she who uses the game of forfeits to humiliate them and to emphasize their blind obedience to her; she who made a kind of playful ritual of stabbing one of them with a pin, foretelling that he would only laugh when she did so, and triumphing in his laughter; this brilliant, gay and, at heart, tender creature, is to submit so abjectly and with such obsessed pleasure to the elder Voldemar that the final scene of the story is that in which the boy, an unseen observer, sees his father strike Zinaïda with his riding-switch. She is at an open window; Vladimir's father, outside the house, is leaning in to her across the sill.

I began to watch; I strained my ears to listen. It seemed as though my father were insisting on something. Zinaïda would not consent. I seem to see her face now — mournful, serious, lovely, and with an inexpressible impress of devotion, grief, love, and a sort of despair — I can find no other word for it. She uttered monosyllables, not raising her eyes, simply smiling — submissively, but without yielding. By that smile alone, I should have known my Zinaïda of old days. My father shrugged his shoulders, and straightened his hat on his head, which was always a sign of impatience with him. . . . Then I caught the words: 'Vous devez vous séparer de cette. . . .' Zinaïda sat up, and stretched out her arm. . . . Suddenly, before my very eyes, the impossible happened. My father suddenly lifted the whip, with which he had been switching the dust off his coat, and I heard a sharp blow on that arm, bare to the elbow. I could scarcely restrain myself from crying out; while Zinaïda shuddered, looked without a word at my father, and slowly raising her arm to her lips, kissed the streak of red upon it. My father flung away the whip, and running quickly up the steps, dashed into the house. . . . Zinaïda turned round, and with out-stretched arms and downcast head, she too moved away from the window.

That, apart from Zinaïda's death, is to be the end of the story.

Now, having looked ahead so far, having seen a little, but as yet by no means all, of what Turgenev is driving at, let us see what his method is and what his attitude of mind is towards love, and how that method and that attitude are peculiar to him and make him the artist that he is.

### 7

His attitude of mind is, first of all, compassionate, and his method gentle. Never was there a man less given to violence of thought or of style. He did not, as the fierce materialists do, divide human beings into abrupt categories to be labelled for perpetual praise or perpetual damnation. There are psychologists who, hearing the tale that I have just outlined — the tale of the face-slapping, the forfeits, the pin and the whip — would say that Turgenev's story was of the masochism and the sadism of passion, and, if they were storytellers, they would tell it in those ugly terms. The idea of setting it in a context of a boy's first love would seem to them utterly false. They would brutalize it in the cause, as they supposed, of naturalistic and materialistic truth, and would despise Turgenev for what they would regard as his avoidances. The question we have to ask is whether they are right or whether his truth is in fact more profound and more genuinely realistic than theirs.

If we are to be fully aware, not only of Turgenev's romantic spell, but of his veracity, it is important to notice two things: that he never allows us to lose sympathy with Zinaïda and yet that he is completely unsparing of her. Enchantment and criticism go hand in hand, as they do in life.

After the game of forfeits, the boy goes home and to his own room. Zinaïda's face floats before him in the darkness. Then the scientific observer in Turgenev smilingly intervenes:

At last I got up, walked on tiptoe to my bed, and without undressing, laid my head carefully on the pillow, as though I were afraid by an abrupt movement to disturb what filled my soul.

But then his father calls at the lodge, and everything begins to change for reasons that the boy does not yet understand. But he understands the cruelty inherent in love.

Zinaïda . . . amused herself with my passion, made a fool of me, petted and tormented me.

She amused herself with her other adorers. She made one of them dress up like a bear and drink salt water. And, though she could not help respecting Lushin, the ironical doctor, she

made him smart for it, and at times, with a peculiar, malignant pleasure, made him feel that he too was at her mercy. 'I'm a flirt, I'm heartless, I'm an actress in my instincts,' she said to him one day in my presence; 'well and good! Give me your hand then; I'll stick this pin in it, you'll be ashamed of this young man's seeing it, it will hurt you, but you'll laugh for all that, you truthful person.'

This unsparing criticism of Zinaïda is followed by the boy's discovery that she herself is beginning to suffer as her victims suffer. It is one of Turgenev's most compassionate scenes:

One day I was walking in the garden beside the familiar fence, and I caught sight of Zinaïda; leaning on both arms, she was sitting on the grass, not stirring a muscle. I was about to make off cautiously, but she suddenly raised her head and beckoned me imperiously. My heart failed me; I did not understand her at first. She repeated her signal. I promptly jumped over the fence and ran joyfully up to her, but she brought me to a halt with a look, and motioned me to the path two paces from her. In confusion, not knowing what to do, I fell on my knees at the edge of the path. She was so pale, such bitter suffering, such intense weariness, was expressed in every feature of her face, that it sent a pang to my heart, and I muttered unconsciously, 'What is the matter?'

Zinaïda stretched out her head, picked a blade of grass, bit it and flung it away from her.

'You love me very much?' she asked at last. 'Yes.'

I made no answer — indeed, what need was there to answer?

'Yes,' she repeated, looking at me as before. 'That's so. The same eyes,' — she went on; sank into thought, and hid her face in her hands. 'Everything's grown so loathsome to me,' she whispered. 'I would have gone to the other end of the world first — I can't bear it, I can't get over it. . . . And what is there before me! . . . Ah, I am wretched. . . . My God, how wretched I am!'

'What for?'

She makes him read poetry to her; then walks with him towards the house.

Zinaïda hurriedly pressed my hand and ran on ahead. We went back into the lodge. Meidanov set to reading us his 'Manslayer', which had just appeared in print, but I did not hear him. He screamed and drawled his four-foot iambic lines, the alternating rhythms jingled like little bells, noisy and meaningless, while I still watched Zinaïda and tried to take in the import of her last words.

> 'Perchance some unknown rival
> Has surprised and mastered thee?'

Meidanov bawled suddenly through his nose — and my eyes and Zinaïda's met. She looked down and faintly blushed. I saw her blush, and grew cold with terror. I had been jealous before, but only at that instant the idea of her being in love flashed upon my mind. 'Good God! she is in love!'

## 8

In episode after episode, Turgenev now develops his theme: that in love (and, therefore, in life itself) as we are, in spite of ourselves, both tyrants and victims, we are little entitled to set ourselves up as judges, and shall certainly be wrong if we try to make creation conform to the rigid pattern of a materialistic orthodoxy. In human nature, motive cannot be divided into compartments, for conflicting motives co-exist in the human heart, and are to be seen *through* one another. This is not, in the popular sense, an optimistic theme. It prescribes no anodyne against suffering nor does it presuppose that by organization we can guarantee happiness to ourselves. But it does presuppose that we live, not in herds under a roof with guards at the door, but in the airs of heaven, and that it is wiser and more just, when lovely woman stoops to folly, to listen to the aeolian music arising from the strings of her individuality and to recognize the beauty of this music, than to destroy all music by the violence of our own screaming. What Turgenev is always seeking is harmony — a harmony which can arise only from recognition, by a sensitive ear, of life's differing notes: a harmony which we hear sometimes, then lose again: a harmony which, if only we ourselves can make ourselves be still and listen, is audible in experience, but which is drowned or converted into chaotic discord if, like the materialists, we shout or whine.

In this spirit he invites us to consider Zinaïda and Vladimir Petrovitch, and even the boy's father. Vladimir Petrovitch is so happily love's fool that when Zinaïda mockingly bids him jump off a fourteen-foot wall, he jumps unhesitatingly and collapses at her feet. As he recovers consciousness, he hears her say: 'How could you do it? How could you obey? You know I love you . . .' and 'her fresh lips began covering my face with kisses . . . they touched my lips.' Is that rapture foolishness in him, or the assurance that she loves him hypocrisy in her? You may answer: 'She loved the father; therefore she was lying to the son'; but she was not lying; she was speaking out of Turgenev's charitable wisdom, out of his acceptance of the infinite complexities of the human heart. Others are satirical; others are ironical; but no one else, I think, has Turgenev's gift of loving irony. Other men condemn first and perhaps forgive afterwards, but the gods and Turgenev observe and forgive *at the same time*. That, perhaps, is why the modern world is beginning to turn to him again.

9

That, perhaps, is why his play, *A Month in the Country*, which is almost a companion piece to *First Love*, was regarded throughout the twenties and thirties as too thinly romantic for commercial production, and why, when at last it was produced during the war at the St. James's Theatre, it drew all England. In this play there is again a story of first love. More important, the elder woman, Natalya, though different from Zinaïda in age and circumstance, is, like Zinaïda, such a woman as Turgenev loved to paint — a woman to whom love comes as a delicious madness, which, though she cannot resist it, she is able, with a detached part of herself, to criticize. Turgenev understood, and was able to express, the truth that passion is a solvent of the barriers set up by conscience and habit between the good and the evil in men. Those who are led by it to folly and misery are to be pitied, not condemned — perhaps not even to be pitied, for is not imaginative life, though it lead to suffering, better than imaginative stagnation, and is not love an imaginative flux? Because he held this view of love — a view which allies it with poetry rather than with morals or biology — he has been accused of being a sentimentalist. But that was not Tolstoy's view of him or Flaubert's. It is a recent view, based upon the abject Marxian philosophy that only matter is real and that all of us, except our flesh, is delusion. Turgenev was, in fact, a realist, and a realist the more profound because his realism, informed by poetic vision, took account of the intangible. His people may appear at first to be creatures of unaccountable mood; but, as we live with them, we begin to understand that all their moods, their contradictions, their changes of mind, spring from his grasp of one over-riding truth: that men, and women even more certainly than men, are capable, not only of motives successive and conflicting, but of wanting and not wanting a thing *at the same instant*. It is this that gives to his love-stories a kind of scintillating elasticity. No one — except a character here and there that is too closely identified with political theory, and these characters are his weakness, not his strength — no one, apart from these, is rooted in opinion. His people are even a little dazzled, as we all are when we are awake, by the kaleidoscope of vision; they dance with truth.

10

Let us then take one last glance at Zinaïda and Vladimir Petrovitch before we part from them. She has become his father's mistress and at last the boy knows it. He has seen them out riding together; he has pursued them into the garden, a jealous Othello with a knife, and at sight of his father has dropped the knife. He is in rapture and despair; so, even more terribly, is she. His family is moving back to Moscow. The summer holiday is over. Vladimir Petrovitch goes to the lodge to say good-bye:

In the drawing-room the old princess met me with her usual slovenly and careless greetings.

'How's this, my good man, your folks are off in such a hurry?' she observed, thrusting snuff into her nose. I looked at her, and a load was taken off my heart. The word 'loan', dropped by Philip, had been torturing me. She had no suspicion . . . at least I thought so then. Zinaïda came in from the next room, pale, and dressed in black, with her hair hanging loose; she took me by the hand without a word, and drew me away with her.

'I heard your voice,' she began, 'and came out at once. Is it so easy for you to leave us, bad boy?'

'I have come to say good-bye to you, princess,' I answered, 'probably for ever. You have heard, perhaps, we are going away.'

Zinaïda looked intently at me.

'Yes, I have heard. Thanks for coming. I was beginning to think I should not see you again. Don't remember evil against me. I have sometimes tormented you, but all the same I am not what you imagine me.'

She turned away, and leaned against the window.

'Really, I am not like that. I know you have a bad opinion of me.'

'I?'

'Yes, you . . . you.'

'I?' I repeated mournfully, and my heart throbbed as of old under the influence of her overpowering, indescribable fascination. 'I? Believe me, Zinaïda Alexandrovna, whatever you did, however you tormented me, I should love and adore you to the end of my days.'

She turned with a rapid motion to me, and flinging wide her arms, embraced my head, and gave me a warm and passionate kiss. God knows whom that long farewell kiss was seeking, but I eagerly tasted its sweetness. I knew that it would never be repeated. 'Good-bye, good-bye,' I kept saying. . . .

She tore herself away, and went out. And I went away. I cannot describe the emotion with which I went away. I should not wish it ever to come again; but I should think myself unfortunate had I never experienced such an emotion.

He never spoke to her again, though he saw her once more on the occasion when his father struck her with a whip. Four years later, hearing that she was in town, he tried to see her again, but went too late. She was already dead.

## II

That is all. What emerges above all else is an impression of beauty and truth. Nothing has been distorted, nothing falsified. The life depicted has been full of suffering, even of waste and folly, and yet it has not been either ugly or in vain. For Turgenev, the material things we touch and measure — even Zinaïda in her grave, 'those dear features, those eyes, those curls, in the narrow box, in the damp underground darkness' — though they may be objectively real, are not the only reality; they are certainly emblems as well as objects, and perhaps emblems only.

Emblems of what? Turgenev is not a dogmatist. He gives no precise answer to that question, but makes us aware that there is an answer. To know that there is an answer is to accept life in the Turgenevian sense, to observe suffering and rapture with an equal eye; not, as a man, to be restive; not, as an artist, to scream. This, I think, is what Tolstoy meant when he said that he valued Turgenev 'just because he is not restive'. Dostoevski, he added, was restive, and so his 'wisdom and heart ran to waste. . . . Turgenev,' Tolstoy declared, 'will outlive Dostoevski, and not for his artistic qualities but because he is not restive.'

12

This story of *First Love* is evidence in support of Tolstoy's verdict. No story is emotionally more highly charged and yet none is less 'restive' or enables us to understand more clearly why a man so different from Tolstoy as Henry James should have spoken of Turgenev as 'the least unsafe man of genius' he had met. I owe that reference to Sir Edmund Spriggs, and I think it is valuable to notice that so distinguished a man of science, in his Harveian Oration delivered before the Royal College of Physicians in 1944, chose Turgenev as an instance of the application to art of the Harveian method.

By the Harveian method (he said) is meant the use of observation and experiment guided by knowledge and thought. Opposed to it is thinking, or accepting what others have said, without the control of looking and trying.

This goes to the root of my contention: that Turgenev, accused by his opponents of being a romantic avoider of the truth, is better equipped than they are, both by his method and by his temperament, to reveal human nature and to inspire those guesses — no less scientific because they are guesses — without which the seeming contradictions of human nature cannot be reconciled. But Turgenev is not a sentimentalist. Hear how he ends his love story:

I remember, a few days after I heard of Zinaïda's death, I was present, through a peculiar, irresistible impulse, at the death of a poor old woman who lived in the same house as we. Covered with rags, lying on hard boards, with a sack under her head, she died hardly and painfully. Her whole life had been passed in the bitter struggle with daily want; she had known no joy, had not tasted the honey of happiness. One would have thought, surely she would rejoice at death, at her deliverance, her rest. But yet, as long as her decrepit body held out, as long as her breast still heaved in agony under the icy hand weighing upon it, until her last forces left her, the old woman crossed herself, and kept whispering, 'Lord, forgive my sins'; and only with the last spark of consciousness, vanished from her eyes the look of fear, of horror of the end. And I remember that then, by the death-bed of that poor old woman, I felt aghast for Zinaïda, and longed to pray for her, for my father — and for myself.

There let us leave it. We have been in the presence of a great artist and a gentle man of whom there is need in this restive, bitter and opinionated world. Unless civilization is utterly destroyed by those whose materialism has brought it to the very edge of madness, Turgenev will become, I think, more and more a contemporary, because a universal and spiritual, force. But it is not for his opinions that he will live. No novelist, not even Tolstoy, lives for his opinions. He will live, as Tolstoy does in *Anna Karenina*, because he knows how to evoke the scent and touch of a woman, and how to love her, and how, like the gods themselves, to forgive her her sins.

He knows how to enable us to re-imagine and to receive into ourselves the uniqueness of each human experience, the solitary miracle of each man's and each woman's being alive: because, for example, he knows, not only how to describe a woman or how to analyse her character, but how to evoke her scent, her touch, her presence, her being she, as in her own heart she is herself and none other; and so, for all her faults, how to love her, and how, in that love, to abstain from judgement of her, and how, not presuming himself to forgive any creature, to pray for her in the same prayer that he prays for himself.

# NELSON

Miss Carola Oman's *Nelson*\* appeared seven years ago. Since then she has published a biography of Sir John Moore. From an historical point of view, the *Moore* is as good as the *Nelson*, as scholarly, as humane and as little likely to be superseded, and yet the admiral, as always, steals the limelight. If we are seeking an outstanding biography of the last ten years, it is upon the *Nelson* that choice must fall.

The reason is, in part, that Nelson's life is felt to have completed itself as Moore's did not. The struggle in which Moore had been engaged went on without him. Pitt also died too soon; Wellington too late. But Nelson's death falls like the last line of a sonnet. Everything is done; everything fulfilled. Time, place and fortune chime together. War continued, but not his war. At sea, nothing but commerce-destroying remained to the enemy. Invasion across the Channel having become impossible, Napoleon was compelled, in the desire to throttle England's trade, to attempt the subjugation of all Europe. To this task, which broke him, he was driven by sea-power. Waterloo was a deferred act of execution; Trafalgar the death-warrant.

This is one reason, the aesthetic reason, for Nelson's being a supreme subject for biography. Another is that he was a

\* *Nelson* by Carola Oman (Hodder & Stoughton, 1947).

mysterious creature, the reconciliation of whose qualities
and defects requires of his biographer a rare amalgam of detachment and insight. Until Miss Oman wrote, it might
have been easily claimed that there was no room for another
book about him. As she herself justly says — and it is
pleasant that she should give no countenance to disparagement of Southey — 'an author who could write' produced
in 1813 'one of the tales that hold children from play and
old men from the chimney corner'. Southey, in brief, had
given immortal currency to the legend. Mahan, Laughton,
Corbett and Callender had said what there was to be said of
the officer. As for the man, that strange admixture of romanticism and plainness which was Nelson, the leader of the
Band of Brothers, the lover of Lady Hamilton, had there not
been enough variations on that difficult theme? Why, then,
another book about Nelson? And yet, when Miss Oman's
biography was published, the need of it was at once ap-
parent. It brought together, and composed into a persuasive
portrait, the legendary, the professional and the personal
aspects of its subject.

Fools have said that Nelson was not a good seaman. Such
is mediocrity's loathing of genius; there were memorable
rabbits who said that Keats was not a good poet. The
answer, in Nelson's case, is threefold: first, that, if he had
not known his job, Jervis would not have tolerated him;
secondly, that if he had been a lucky pretender his captains
would not have followed him blind or with their eyes open;
thirdly, that his quality as an officer was the quality hardest
of all to understand in an armchair — the quality of timing.
His 'patent bridge' at St. Vincent may have been, if any
would have it so, the reward of toughness, courage, rashness,
luck, but his initial action in turning the *Captain* out of the

line to challenge and hold an escaping enemy was, against all timid convention, masterly.

It was at this point (says Miss Oman) that a 74, third from the rear of the British line, altered course to the west and threw her-self in defiance across the bows of the Spaniards. An independent squadron was needed in this position, to prevent the battle degenerating into the 'half-begotten' engagement despised by Jervis; and Nelson, with the *Captain*, had resolved to represent it, offering himself to the attack of at least seven enemy sail-of-the-line. He wore out of his station, and came into close action with the *Santissima Trinidad*, largest fighting ship in the world. In quitting the line he was aware that he was not only acting without orders, he was deliberately disobeying them.

His action, if it had failed — that is to say, if it had been wrongly timed — would have been unforgivable. But

I was immediately joined, and most nobly supported, by the *Culloden*, Captain Troubridge. . . . For near an hour, I believe (but do not pretend to be correct as to time), did the *Culloden* and *Captain* support this apparently, but not really, unequal con-test; when the *Blenheim*, passing between us and the enemy, gave us a respite and sickened the Dons.

Miss Oman sees the point. 'Jervis,' she writes, 'having seen and recognized the brilliance of Nelson's action, had ordered the *Excellent*, last ship of the line, to support him instantly. . . .' Instantly is the key-word. It always is where Nelson is concerned. If he had worn out of the line a little sooner or a little later, his adventure would have been either meaning-less or disastrous. As it was, it gave to Jervis's plan the advantage of the clock.

In all matters of seamanship and command, Miss Oman is discerning and quick to the point. A reader who wishes to appreciate the risk Nelson took at the Nile, or the nature of his failure at Santa Cruz, or the brilliance of his success at

Copenhagen is given all the materials of judgement. The narrative of Copenhagen, which includes the full text of Nelson's letter to Sir Hyde Parker before the battle, is particularly useful in proof of professional ability and grasp, but the little anecdote of the signal and the blind eye is there too — for once accurately told. The battle of Cape St. Vincent is described, as it should be by Nelson's biographer, from his point of view, but proportionately and without neglect of Jervis's achievement; and the treatment of Trafalgar is admirably straightforward, well-balanced and moving in its plainness. An historian, with a knowledge of the subject as complete as that which Miss Oman possesses, must have been tempted again and again, particularly in the set-pieces, to exceed the province of biography and to fall into highly technical discussions of tactics and strategy proper to naval history of a different kind. She refrains with unerring judgement. The set-pieces are vivid and unhurried; they are enthralling to read and are given their just place in Nelson's professional achievement; but the long intervals between them are not sacrificed for their sake, and the reader is given an impression of the whole sweep of Nelson's career, of its tedium as well as its triumphs, such as he will receive nowhere else.

So it happens that though Miss Oman, unlike some of her predecessors, does not presume to read lessons to Nelson on his conduct of the sea-affair, and does not even, in her own person, eulogize him, a critical study of the admiral emerges, and we are enabled to observe, as though we were sailing with him, how astonishingly personal and impetuous Nelson was, even in strictly naval matters, as Jervis was not, and how maddening he must have been to Hotham or to Keith who had not the confidence in his genius which Jervis had.

It was Nelson's disconcerting power of suddenly knowing what no text-book could teach which led certain critics to consider him unsound. There was always an undercurrent of professional opinion against him. Some of it was prompted by jealousy; some by what young Lord Elgin called his vain-glory; but by no means all. And it is one of the principal values of the present biography that it proves Nelson's effi-ciency as well as his genius. He was an artist, but a craftsman too. Always on edge and living on his nerves, capable of black discouragement if his intuition played him false as it seemed to have done when he found Alexandria empty, he had yet a great reserve of experience and resolution to sus-tain him. He was hungry for opportunities to exercise a transcendent power of which he did not pretend to be unaware; he had a passion for attack and a boldness which it seems to have been necessary to love if one was not to fear them; and yet nowhere, except at Santa Cruz, did he allow impatience to disturb judgement.

The problem of the man is even more delicate than that of the officer and cannot be separated from it; nor can either be separated from the legend. In these pages, because they never lose touch with the English or the European back-ground to the fleet's activity, one feels the legend grow, and yet it is as impossible to account for it fully and rationally as it is to account for the upspringing of any other deeply per-sonal myth. We may argue with reason that Nelson was a greater man than any of his contemporary admirals, but the difference between his achievement and that of Hood or Jervis does not account for the magic which invested his name even before the Nile and was wholly absent from theirs. The difference is the inexplicable difference between love and admiration. The relationship between Nelson and his men (Miss Oman quotes the written tributes to him that they would leave about on deck) and between him and his officers was highly emotional. Even disapproval of his connexion with Lady Hamilton and the Court of the Two Sicilies was not, as it might well have been, coldly and professionally censorious; it was emotional and jealous. To put it simply, his fleet loved him, and so in the mass did his fellow-countrymen. To attempt to explain the Nelson myth is to attempt to explain love.

Certainly he was conscious of it and may be accused of having cultivated it, but even the cultivation was intuitive. His love of full-dress and decorations, of appearances on balconies, of ceremonial drives, of wreaths and swords and jewels, of all the paraphernalia of 'vainglory', arose, not from cold calculation, but from the fact that life for him was never drab but always tragical or radiant, and sometimes both. A naval officer, who worshipped Nelson, once said to the present writer: 'No one was ever a better hand at a death-scene, and, what is more, he was always prepared to play it'. Miss Oman, recording the incident of his being hit at the Nile, gives his first words 'I am killed. Remember me to my wife', and describes how 'he proceeded to carry everything in the high style dear to him and to Shakespeare', how the Chaplain was summoned, how all the appropriate messages were sent, how his Flag-Captain visited the cockpit with news of victory, and how, in spite of the Surgeon's assurances that he was in no danger, 'the son of the Rector of Burnham Thorpe, struck on the head and in total darkness at last, could not believe that this was not the end'. There is no denying that it reads like a rehearsal for Trafalgar, but it would need an uncommonly mean debunker to snigger at Nelson for that reason. Miss Oman does nothing of the kind.

Her view of Nelson's greatness is steady and unswerving, and is not dimmed even by her candid and detailed account of the period in which he was 'inactive at a foreign court'. She recognizes now and then, by an affectionately ironic turn of phrase, that 'the son of the Rector of Burnham Thorpe' did not suffer from an over-developed sense of humour, but she knows that, if he had, he would have been less than Nelson. There is really no good reason that a great man, who is also something of a child, should keep his ribbons and stars in a bottom drawer, or that he should die in the hour of victory as though he were buying a third-single to Clapham Junction.

If Nelson had been willing to do, if indeed he had been capable of doing, any such thing, there would have been no myth — and no victories in his kind. He was loved and legendary precisely because he carried 'everything in the high style dear to him and to Shakespeare'. Those who made up what he called 'high life' in England were often suspicious of him. At first, Lady Spencer, 'who was determined that her husband's tenure of office (the Admiralty) should be marked by brilliancy and high moral tone, was undecided whether Nelson was an idiot or a genius'. Fortunately she allowed the alternative; but there was always something in Nelson himself — and not only in his want of family influence on the highest level — that alarmed the great and good, except Minto, and made them conspicuously reluctant to allow him to command-in-chief. To us it seems exceedingly odd that he won Copenhagen as second to Hyde Parker, but it did not seem odd, but only uncomfortable, to Hyde Parker. One begins in the end to feel sorry for the worthy men of common fibre who served over Nelson, as one feels sorry for the unfortunates to whom a

o

Brontë came as a governess. Miss Oman writes with so much understanding not of her man only but of the age in which he lived that she is able, without romanticism or anti-romanticism, to indicate genius in terms of fact, and to enable the reader to warm his hands in the glow of Nelson without being blinded by it to his background.

# AN OLD NOVEL RE-BORN *

A NOVELIST may, perhaps, be allowed to suggest that philosophers sometimes take too little account of certain novels which, though not philosophical in a specialist's sense, are not pastimes only but contributions to humane letters. Such novels, long after they have ceased to be fashionable, are re-born in a few minds of each successive generation because they raise questions independent of fashion. An example is Shorthouse's *John Inglesant* which no modern critic discusses, which is certainly not what is ordinarily meant by a popular classic, which has indeed not been heard of by a great many intelligent readers of fiction, but which, nevertheless, as the publishers' marking of its reprints shows, has never ceased to be read. The reason, put shortly, is that *Inglesant* is concerned with quietism, and quietism is one of the profound impulses of the human mind. The novel to be spoken of now is concerned with acceptance, not a popular idea among totalitarians or among self-assertive democrats, but an idea which, if it be understood in a positive sense and distinguished from indifferentism and sloth, is a saving one in a world where even virtue has become largely empirical and relative, and the concept of absolute value has fallen, so to speak, out of the public domain.

* Contributed to *The Hibbert Journal.* April 1949.

# I

Eugène Fromentin's *Dominique* has never made its way among the English-speaking peoples, greatly to their loss. The appearance of a new and sensitive translation * may lead to its becoming more widely known not in England only but in the United States. It is difficult in England today to launch such a book for the same reasons which make it difficult to launch a novel by a new, young writer whose qualities are not modish in either the intellectual or the popular sense. In the past, a writer of distinction, even if he were unknown and swimming against the fashionable tide, would find his book discussed *at length* in the great dailies and weeklies. Space, which now seems fabulous, was given to the discussion of literature, so that a novel which won no wide public for itself might nevertheless prove to be the seed of an increasing repute. That space is no longer available. Nine or ten books are herded together into half a column once a week. It is seldom that anything more than the crudest account of a book and the baldest statement of opinion concerning it can be given; and yet it remains true that the work of a genuinely original young writer, if it is to make its way, needs to be analysed, understood and interpreted at length by a critic who has already his own public familiar with his critical method — a public, that is to say, regular enough and intelligent enough to be able to read between the lines into the very heart of the book criticized. Only in this way can new and strange talent be launched, or an old book which, like *Dominique*, has not a smartly fashionable appearance, be brought to the attention of those who would value it. That they are many, I do not doubt.

* By Sir Edward Marsh (The Cresset Press, 1948).

It may at first seem contradictory to say that this novel 'has not a smartly fashionable appearance', and, in the same breath, that there are many thousands of readers who, if it came into their hands, would value it. This seeming contradiction is to be explained partly by the nature of the book itself and partly by its history.

Fromentin was born at La Rochelle in 1820 and died unexpectedly of an anthrax infection in 1876. During his lifetime he was even more celebrated as a painter than as a writer, though his two books of North African travel, his work on the Old Masters of the Low Countries, *Les Maîtres d'Autrefois*, and his single novel, were recognized by his contemporaries as writing of high rank. Today it is by the novel that his name lives, for it is a recognized small classic of French literature. How this has come about is of great interest, for the history of *Dominique*'s reputation not only throws light upon the problem of literary fashion but explains what was meant just now by saying that, contrary to the fashionable appearances of our own day, the present is a propitious time for sending it out to find English readers.

## II

The simple truth is that, in France, *Dominique* started late, and, in English, desperately later. Though the restraints of its style are classical, its subject and its confessional method give it an air of belonging to the Romantic Movement, and the Romantic Movement, though by no means dead, had long ago ceased to be a fashionable excitement when *Dominique* began to appear in the *Revue des Deux Mondes* on April 15, 1862. The readers of that august periodical appear to have taken very little interest in it — so little indeed that the *Revue* became alarmed; Fromentin was hard-pressed to abridge the later instalments, and there were, according to Edmond Scherer who had it from the novelist himself, anxious discussions as to whether to continue publication to the end. George Sand greeted the story with enthusiasm while it was appearing serially. Flaubert, either then or a little later (his letter is undated), read it at a sitting between eight at night and two in the morning. 'I am burning with desire to see you,' he wrote, 'to talk about it and to congratulate you.' The praises of the elect were not wanting, but neither as a serial nor as a volume did *Dominique* set the Seine on fire.

For this there were two reasons: first, the fashionable and relatively unimportant one that, if it was to excite the smart drawing-rooms and the pseudo-intellectual back-parlours, *Dominique* should have been published twenty years before, and not five years after, *Madame Bovary*; second, the more serious reason, arising from Fromentin's method, that his novel was felt to be, and may still be considered, slow in movement, lacking in action and incident. It is worth while, if we are prepared to take an objective view of our own prejudices, to consider what critical validity these two handicaps have in our own day.

The influence of *Madame Bovary* was gigantic, and rightly so, for it is one of the great novels of the world, but it was often applauded for the wrong reasons, and still is. It was, in fact, a criticism of the distortions produced by Romanticism when applied to life by a woman of unbalanced and exorbitant mind. It might equally have been a criticism of the distortions produced by any other philosophy of life when similarly misapplied. Unless we remember that Flaubert also wrote *Bouvard et Pécuchet*, we cannot understand

*Madame Bovary*, which was not a partisan attack upon the philosophy of Romanticism as such, but a criticism of the stupidities, the inaccuracies, and what Flaubert considered the essential mediocrity of the human mind. The proof that Flaubert's masterpiece was not intended as a 'naturalistic' text-book and that Flaubert himself was as much a romantic as a naturalist is to be found in the whole body of his work and in the unescapable fact that Emma Bovary herself glows. For all her faults and follies, she is never dry as the women of the professional anti-romantics are dry or harsh or dusty. She has sap and — let us use the word deliberately in spite of what the films have done to it — glamour. *Madame Bovary* is not an anti-romantic novel, but a novel written by a romantic with his eyes open.

For that reason, while the fashionable Bovaryists were shrugging their shoulders at *Dominique* because their anti-romantic snobbism told them that they ought not to approve it, Flaubert himself was sitting up all night to read it. If they had read his letter to Fromentin, they would all have made haste to raise embarrassed cheers, just as in our own day, when T. S. Eliot praised Kipling, all the fashionable anti-Kiplingists suddenly turned over in bed. Fashion in literature is always a vice of the timid fellow-travellers, never of the great men. A few years ago, Victor Hugo was 'out' in France; now he is a god again. Today, it is fashionable in Paris to say that the plays of Musset are admissible but that his poems are not; and yet every sane man knows that his poetry, and particularly his *Ode to Malibran*, is indestructible. Today, all but the first-rate talk of Anatole France with disparagement, and yet nothing is more certain than that, in a few years, those who now despise him will be chattering about his flawless prose. Fashion in literature is absurd; the masters, from Donne to Meredith, from Meredith to Kipling, from Baudelaire to Poe, always survive it; but it is temporarily formidable, and *Dominique* was held back by it. Today, there is no reason that it should be held back among us, as it was when an earlier English translation appeared in 1932. The 'thirties marked the height of our own anti-romantic movement, but today even the cult of violence is almost spent, and whoever can listen to Chopin can read Fromentin.

## III

And yet the parallel is inexact. Chopin, within the discipline of his form, had an urgency and a pressure that Frometin had not. He himself spoke of his '*lenteurs*', and the criticism of *Dominique* as slow-moving is justifiable. If it were to take rank as a love-story with Turgenev's *First Love* or *Torrents of Spring*, its narrative would have been strung, as Turgenev's narrative is, on quiet but lively incident, and character would have emerged, not primarily from analysis, but from luminous dialogue and action. But this is to say only that Fromentin had his limitations. The real question is: what use did he make of them? To say that he was not Turgenev is to use a form of comparative criticism which, though it may be interesting and sometimes illuminating, can easily be carried so far that it becomes sterile. Instead of saying what an author was not, instead of describing him in his relationship to other authors and to schools and tendencies, can we say what, in himself, he was? What was the peculiarity, the identity, of Fromentin? What is the uniqueness of *Dominique*?

Suddenly the word 'uniqueness', used almost by chance in the sentence just written, emerges as the key-word in any criticism of *Dominique*. Unique does not mean rare, exceptional, unusual; it means, by the dictionary: 'of which there is only one; one and only; single, sole, solitary'. In that strict sense of the word, Fromentin's novel is unique. There are greater novels, but there is none in the same kind with it, just as there are greater books than Trelawny's *Recollections of Shelley and Byron*, but there is none in the same kind with it. Attempts are sometimes made by those who cannot be happy until they have sorted everything into categories to herd *Dominique*, as an autobiographical novel, into the same pen with Constant's *Adolphe* and even with Rousseau's *Nouvelle Héloïse*, but it will not do. The differences are overwhelmingly greater than the likenesses. In its merits and its demerits, *Dominique* stands alone.

Its story is by no means unique, not even exceptional. Dominique, when very young, falls in love with Madeleine, a little older than himself. She marries another before Dominique has declared his love to her or even to himself. Rapture, melancholy, torment and frustration follow. Dominique tries to cure himself by solitude and work, then by taking a mistress who has no impact upon him and passes across the novel as a nameless shadow. Next he tries by being continually in Madeleine's company to convert love into friendship, and she, wishing to help him, makes a corresponding attempt. All in vain. Passion is contagious. Instead of curing him, she herself falls passionately in love with him. For them there is no remedy but to part for ever, she to continue in her marriage, he to find at last, as the husband of another and admirable woman, tranquillity in the countryside where he was born. Where, it may be asked, is the 'uniqueness' of that? Is not the tale, in its outline, familiar enough?

Yes: but it is familiar neither in its motive nor in its method. Consider its method first. It begins with an account of Dominique as an ageing man living, with his wife and children, a retired life at Les Trembles, his country estate on the border of the Bay of Biscay. This is a long prologue, and a brief epilogue reverts to the same scene. In between is Dominique's own narrative of his boyhood, of his love for Madeleine, of his life with her and without her in the country and in Paris, and of the final crisis and parting.

George Sand, one of the book's friendliest critics, recognized that the opening was slow but also that it was too beautiful to be cut. Instead, she wanted the end to be elaborated, partly to give better proportion to the book, partly because she felt that the transition between Dominique's parting from Madeleine and our discovery of him tranquilly married to another woman, of whom we know almost nothing, was too abrupt. Rightly or wrongly, Fromentin, though he accepted minor revisions from her, disregarded her structural advice; rightly, we may believe, not because the advice itself was bad — on the contrary, it was extremely good — but because it was external to him, and he could not have given effect to it without destructive artificiality. The result is a book less competent than George Sand would have made it, but, for that reason the more, Fromentin's very own.

## IV

Its 'slowness', its lack of incident and dialogue, may be seen, from another point of view, as an extreme dramatic economy. No writer knows better than Fromentin how to stop when he has made his point. For example, he describes with beautiful care a scene in a lighthouse. Dominique and his friend Olivier, Madeleine and her young sister Julie, who loves Olivier with hopeless, unrequited love, are on the platform gazing into the abyss.

I knew instinctively that the tension was too great: sooner or later a string would snap. One of us would break down — perhaps not the one who was most deeply moved, but the one with least power of resistance. It was Julie.

Fromentin then tells how giddiness took her, how she almost fell, how Olivier put his arms round her. Then:

A few seconds later she came to, with a sigh of distress that heaved the thin stuff of her bodice. 'It's nothing,' she said, reacting immediately from the fit of weakness that had been too much for her, and down we went.

Flaubert might have cut: 'reacting immediately from the fit of weakness that had been too much for her'. It is debatable. Otherwise, the passage is flawless.

The same economy appears even in the scene of Madeleine and Dominique's final parting:

It was nearly ten when Madeleine came down. . . .
'Father,' she said, in a fearless and resolute tone, ' I want to be alone with M. de Bray for a moment.'
He got up without demur, and left us, giving her a fatherly kiss.
'You are going away tomorrow,' she said. We were both standing.
'Yes,' I replied.
'And we shall never see one another again.'
I made no answer.
'Never,' she repeated. 'Do you understand? Never. I've put between us the only barrier which neither of us could ever dream of passing.'

By this, she means her admission of passion in herself, her acknowledgement that their continued meeting could now be only a prelude to mortal sin. Nothing is harder to communicate in a novel than this quality of absolute resolve that makes argument superfluous and qualification a surrender. Fromentin communicates it with a finality and simplicity of language equal to the cause.

His method has another quality peculiar to him which is an integral part of what is called his slowness. It has been said that he was a painter. In particular, he was a landscapist. It is therefore not surprising that he should have seen the background of his story with a painter's eye, but it is remarkable that, having this pictorial power, he was able to transcend it, to transmute it to serve his narrative purpose. When he describes a natural scene, as when he tells of a dramatic action, he writes always quietly, with economy, proclaiming no emotion, avoiding over-emphasis at all costs. And yet his descriptions of nature are a part of his dramatic method. Through them he communicates the moods, the sufferings, the delights and, above all, the tensions of his characters. In this special power, he has no superior, and takes rank even with Turgenev in his *Sportsman's Sketches*. The most ignorant townsman, who can find none of the pleasures of familiarity in descriptions of rural scenes, may be enthralled by Fromentin in this vein, for it is in his descriptions of nature that he continually reveals the essence of his characters. When Madeleine is lost and Dominique is returning to his old home, 'hurrying on my miserable journey like a wounded animal losing blood and struggling to reach its hole before its strength gives out', Fromentin describes the young man's walk across the solitary marshes, 'the peculiar rushing, rustling sound of wild-duck overhead', and his encounter with an old servant out shooting. It is a description not only of great beauty but of astonishing evocative power. It is too precious to abbreviate, too long to quote at length. Perhaps quotation is unnecessary.

That little phrase about a wounded animal losing blood is evidence enough that, as a country poet, a country dramatist, Fromentin is unique.

## V

His book is unique also in its motive. He has something to say about love and the responsibilities arising from it which has not been said elsewhere; and what he says about love has its bearing upon the whole conduct of life — upon all our hungers and not only upon that of desire; upon all our dedications and loyalties, and not only upon those of love; upon all our confusions, our deadlocks, our tormented oppositions of right to right, our cry that 'nothing makes sense!' A few years ago, no cry was more frequent among the contradictions and frustrations of the contemporary world. The despair and the self-pity implied in it were characteristic of the novel of violence (i.e. of anarchy) and of a formidable body of verse that shouted and whimpered but did not sing. Upon all this Fromentin makes his unique comment.

He assumes the existence and the over-riding validity of an absolute value which is not happiness. He assumes, further, that happiness itself cannot be obtained except by those who recognize this over-riding value. In the particular instance given by the novel, the concrete form of this absolute value happens to be the indissolubility of marriage, but the point of the novel is not to argue for this indissolubility, though the virtue of it is implied, but rather to suggest that life is unlivable in a world reduced to chaos by each man's and each woman's supposing that every impediment to his or her personal satisfaction is an intolerable injustice entitling him or her to break it down if possible and, in case of failure, to cry out: 'Nothing makes sense!' We may, if we will, disagree with Fromentin on the subject of marriage if we accept other absolutes, belief in God or courage in battle or the sacredness of our given word — *something* from which we will not swerve in quest of our own ease or pleasure.

Fromentin, in effect, says: 'No. Your unhappiness, even though it spring from no fault of yours, does not entitle you to take sides with chaos. Life which is not lived within a rule of law is not life, but death.' When, near the end of the book, Madeleine's and Dominique's love is fully recognized by them both, and Dominique, knowing that she is awake within, has come as far as her bedroom door, he turns away, not because it is expedient to do so, not in any consideration of conventional honour, but in obedience to an absolute law which is of the essence of Fromentin's story:

... Here I was, groping my way about the sleeping, unsuspecting house, in the middle of the night, drawn irresistibly to Madeleine's bedroom door, and bumping against it like a man in a dream. Was I merely an unhappy being with nothing left to sacrifice, blinded by desire, neither better nor worse than the rest of my fellow-creatures? or was I a criminal? This crucial question floated vaguely at the back of my mind without leading me to anything remotely resembling a positive choice between the alternatives of behaving like a man of honour, and deliberately planning an infamy. All that I knew beyond a doubt — and even that left me undecided — was that if Madeleine sinned it would kill her and that most certainly I shouldn't survive her an hour.

I can't tell you what saved me. All I know is that I found myself in the park. ...

The important sentence is: '*La seule chose dont je ne doutais pas ... c'est qu'une faute tuerait Madeleine.*' The novel rests upon that basis of absolutism. Sainte-Beuve, who was prevented by the limitations of his genius from recognizing absolutism when he saw it, while praising the novel on all other grounds, objected to this *dénouement* which, he said, was not *entièrement d'accord avec la verité humaine*. He thought — and it is typical of Sainte-Beuve — that Madeleine would have had good reason to despise Dominique for having brought her so far and then drawn back, and Dominique himself, according to Sainte-Beuve, was a halfhearted lover 'who mistook his natural timidity for stoicism'. It is one of those unseeing and would-be worldly-wise comments which, in the work of a critic so masterly and so discerning on his own territory, make one blink. It misses the whole point of the book, which consists in its assumption that it was not open to the two lovers to argue with their appetites or to compromise with their separation. Their struggle from beginning to end is not to find a way round the truth as they see it, not to pride themselves on their stoicism or to despise each other for their abstentions, not to submit themselves to their satisfactions but to liberate themselves by their acceptances. It is this that Sainte-Beuve could not see when he wrote in 1864 and that we might not have been able to see in 1934. But today, when society is in peril of dissolving because the rejection of absolute values has resulted in chaos and chaos in violence, when we have come — to use Sainte-Beuve's words — *jusqu'au bord extrême du précipice*, we know that there are moments in life when it is necessary to stand absolutely and when '*une faute tuerait Madeleine*'. That this is an enduring truth, independent of fashion, is a reason for *Dominique*'s survival through eighty years of tragedy in France. That it is a present truth, of mounting urgency in our own day, is a reason for thinking that there is a vast modern audience who would find their own intuitions of wisdom crystallized in Fromentin's story.

*Printed in Great Britain*
*by Richard Clay and Company, Ltd.,*
*Bungay, Suffolk*